D0096986

STORIES OF PARADISE

STORIES OF PARADISE

The Study of Classical and Modern Autobiographies of Faith

by

Louis John Cameli

PAULIST PRESS
New York, N.Y./Ramsey, N.J.

ACKNOWLEDGMENTS

Grateful acknowledgment is made to the publishers indicated for their kind permission to quote from the following works:

Scripture texts are taken from the *New American Bible*, copyright © 1970, by the Confraternity of Christian Doctrine, Washington, D.C. All rights reserved.

The Seven Story Mountain by Thomas Merton. New York, Harcourt, Brace Jovanovich, Inc., 1948. Used with permission.

Story of a Soul: The Autobiography of St. Thérèse of Lisieux, trans. by John Clarke, O.C.D. Washington, D.C., ICS Publications, 1975. Used with permission.

Copyright © 1978 by
The Missionary Society
of St. Paul the Apostle
in the State of New York

All rights reserved. No part of this book may be reproduced or transmitted in any form or by any means, electronic or mechanical, including photocopying, recording or by any information storage and retrieval system without permission in writing from the Publisher.

Library of Congress
Catalog Card Number: 78-58961

ISBN: 0-8091-2130-1

Published by Paulist Press
Editorial Office: 1865 Broadway, New York, N.Y. 10023
Business Office: 545 Island Road, Ramsey, N.J. 07446

Printed and bound in the
United States of America

CONTENTS

*To the students of the seminary
and the people in the parishes
who trusted me with their stories*

PREFACE

In *Stories of Paradise*, I have attempted to draw together some intuitions about spirituality as a study, and as a formative process. I hope that readers will be led to pursue some of the primary sources of spirituality with an appreciation of the relevance of those sources for their own spiritual stories, as well as the stories of others.

Spirituality is in vogue today. If the interest in spirituality is to be sustained, and if such interest is to contribute to a fuller and deeper living of the Christian life, then we must find ways of seriously and critically reflecting on spirituality. Furthermore, the insights generated from a serious study of spirituality ought to contribute to practical ways of helping people today to grow in spiritual life. *Stories of Paradise*, then, represents one attempt to meet the double need to pursue spirituality as study, and as formation.

Readers will benefit most from this book when they read it in conjunction with the four autobiographies indicated in the text and in the reading references on pages 85–86.

A word of thanks is owed to many people; colleagues and friends who helped and encouraged me. In a special way, I thank the students who have taken my courses on spirituality by way of autobiography and spiritual direction. Their questions and interest have sharpened my perceptions of spirituality.

CHAPTER ONE

AN INTRODUCTION

Stories of Paradise

Once there was a village. It lay nestled in the mountains of a distant kingdom. Nature gifted the village with striking beauty for its setting, fertile soil, and plenteous water which was clear and pure. Far more remarkable, however, were the inhabitants of the village. They lived good lives. Neighbor cared for neighbor. Justice loomed high as the mountains, and peace ran through their lives like the clear currents of the rivers.

The Lord God smiled on the village. He was well pleased by his sons and daughters. Indeed, the Lord was so pleased by the village that he sent two angels to the villagers to announce a great favor.

The angels spoke to the villagers and said: "You have pleased the Lord your God. He wants you to begin to build and to enjoy paradise in your very own village." The people were astonished. "But you must select four people," they continued, "to visit the Lord's paradise in heaven. Having seen the Lord's paradise in heaven, they will be able to tell you how to build his paradise in your village." The excited villagers immediately selected four people: a hunter, a cook, a farmer, and a builder. The angels of the Lord transported them to the paradise of heaven.

The sight of paradise entranced them. They saw before them a large rich garden. Animals of every sort abounded. There were deer and fat quail. Fruit trees laden with ripe fruit dotted the garden. Precious herbs and spices grew wild. Fields ready for a bountiful harvest of wheat and corn surrounded the garden. In the midst of the garden stood a magnificent house, beautifully built and containing dwellings for all God's children.

When the four village representatives returned to the village, they could barely utter a word. But their fellow villagers pressed them to describe paradise, and how they might build it in their own village. The hunter began. "Paradise," he said, "is like a large game preserve which is richly stocked. If we would have paradise, we must stock our forests with deer and quail." The cook spoke next. She said, "Paradise contains all good things to cook and eat. If we would have paradise, we must grow fruits and herbs and spices." Then the farmer spoke. "Paradise is always ready for an abundant harvest. If we would have paradise, we must plant all our fields." Finally the builder spoke. "Paradise contains a matchless house, utterly spacious and richly furnished to house all God's children. If we would have paradise, we must build such a house." The speakers melted into the silent memory of paradise in heaven. But the villagers were completely bewildered.

"What is paradise really like?" they asked each other. They knew the four speakers to be good and honest. Yet each one gave a different picture of paradise. Caught in their dilemma, the villagers could not begin to build paradise, because they did not know what to build. They had no one picture of paradise in heaven.

After a while, a wise elder of the village stood up. He said, "My people do not be discouraged. Let us listen again to these stories of paradise. Even if they are different, perhaps they are not apart." Once again the four speakers told of paradise as they had before. When they had finished, a silence came over the village. All waited with a deep desire to know and to build paradise. Then, the elder who had spoken before broke the silence. He cried out, "They are one! They are one!" People asked him, "What is one?" He replied, "They are one story, a story of abundance. There is plenty of game, vast quantities of food, rich harvests, and a spacious house. It is abundance." Now, the villagers knew and they began to build.

The Village Today

The stories of paradise capture today's mood of spirituality. People experience a great promise, a hope of renewal in themselves and the world. But when they reach for the promise, it melts into a bewildering multiplicity of claims of experience and suggested methods of development. One speaks of the charismatic experience and the need to form prayer groups. Another urges us to return to the mystics of our tradition and to learn from them how to experience God. Yet another wants us to tap the riches of the Eastern spiritual tradition so that we can learn to breathe and meditate and touch the Infinite. And so on.

Standing before these many claimants and hearing their voices, we cannot form a single picture of spiritual renewal. We are stopped and perhaps wary of opting for a fad or, worse, an escape. Unlike the villagers, we have no wise elder who cracks the riddle of many stories about one thing.

Uneasiness does not stop with the perplexing multiplicity of claims in the village itself. A thought menaces the villagers today. Perhaps they hunch over their many plans for paradise in solemn isolation from the rest of the kingdom. Perhaps they belong to the fringe. Perhaps, they haltingly surmise, they are out of it.

The village situation today bewilders and immobilizes us, but it may also cause us to scan the situation and to listen once again to the stories of paradise. The urgency which generates hope in the promise of spiritual renewal can lead us, if not to a single word solution, at least out of immobility.

The urgency of a renewal of spirituality has many roots today. Two dimensions are particularly weighty and mobilizing. One is theological, the other is pastoral-formational.

Theologians today invest heavily in the work of fundamental theology. They speak of faith and how it is a reasonable human choice, and how it is or can be coherent with the experience of living in today's world. Even when theologians present the dialectical or shattering character of faith in the face of contemporary human experience, they cannot escape their partner in dialog, a secular experience which presumes no religious faith. Theologians strive to work out foundations of belief, or to reinterpret in fundamental ways elements of faith tradition with a singular purpose. They explore the truth of faith, but not as a naked truth. Their purpose is to expose a meaningful truth which is therefore also central to life.

The world does not hang on religious faith to build its cities, to do medical research, to develop agrotechnology, to govern states. Far more devastating than religious persecutions, which acknowledge a worthy opponent for battle, is the polite hush on faith talk or God talk, a hush which shunts these concerns to the periphery. In

the face of this peripheral displacement, theologians labor strenu-
ously to ground the possibility of faith in today's world. The work,
involving mazes of intricate analysis, pushes ahead as if driven by
one often unspoken energy—the quest for the center.

Theologians from the time of Clement of Alexandria have
endeavored to dialog with their culture, and not simply to gain a
position, but to preach faith to people both within and without the
community of faith who experience special needs for reasonable-
ness and coherence. That task must continue. At the same time,
some theologians see possibilities for breakthroughs in a com-
plementary type of study. Several theologians, for example, at the
1976 meeting of the Catholic Theological Society of America con-
cluded their presentations with an appeal, either direct or indirect,
to study the spiritual experience of writers in our tradition. Louis
Dupré, and his two respondents, David Burrell and Anne Carr,
agreed that a truly significant avenue for understanding and presenting the interdependence between creator and creature could be
found in the experience of intimate union described by spiritual
writers who themselves had the experience. The program of study
proposed by Dupré and others recommends not abandoning a
theological-analytical approach, but complementing that approach
by entering and probing the lived faith experience as accessible to
us in its heightened and crystallized forms. Entrance into such
primary faith experience promises material for theological elaboration as well as, it is hoped, a self-validating presentation of religious
faith's centrality to life.

Exposition of the spiritualities, or the spiritual stories, of particular people speak with a unique force to believers and unbeliev-
ers alike. That force or energy contained in the personal accounts
bespeaks a forceful and energizing center of life that wells up into
inadequate words, but works in their lives a transformation of life
itself. At that point, the theologians and the spiritual story tellers
converge in their efforts to give witness to the source and center of
life.

Many and, at times, confusing voices urge and promise spiritual renewal. The many "stories of paradise," which are multiple
claims of spiritual experience and methods, cause us to stop and
wait and wonder where to go. Current theological endeavors do not
provide an answer. They do, however, underline the urgency of

moving out of immobility and studying the experiences themselves. The urgency of the theologians derives from the insightful and honest recognition of the limits of an intellectual analysis of life in faith. A different but related set of concerns also underscores the urgency of exploring spiritual stories. These are pastoral-formational.

The observations on pastoral-formational needs are personal. They reflect my experience as well as the experience of others who have been, or are presently, involved in pastoral ministry. A more rigorously scientific and empirically based analysis would, I believe, substantiate these observations.

People involved in pastoral ministry quickly perceive that religious institutions and religious life in general serve some basic human needs. Religion provides individual and social resources. Religion furnishes the individual with an effective resource for coping. In a framework of beliefs, hopes, and rituals, religion offers massive assistance to the individual who must deal with the enigmas and joys of human life. Suffering, pain, anxiety, success, joy, growth, all find in religion, if not an answer, then at least a symbolic resonance which pulls the individual out of unmanageable isolation. What I face in life, I do not face uniquely or alone. My traditions inform me and encourage me as I confront a termination in death, or a new beginning in marriage. Others have gone before me in these paths. Others walk with me at this very moment. So, religion provides a resource for coping. But if "coping" sounds too narrow and negative, religion, it should also be noted, gives a plan for human development or, in Abraham Maslow's terms, "self-actualization." I can become the good person I am destined and called to become. I have a program and indications and others to guide me.

In addition, religion grounds a possibility for a social context. The human "belonging" need finds a response in religious life and institutions. People can find each other in a framework of shared beliefs, hopes, and rituals. These elements serve not simply to identify where the group is or how one can join it; they also continue to bind the group together.

Pastoral ministers feel uneasy when they clearly recognize these uses of religion, especially if the uses are the only purpose behind religious affiliation and involvement. People who only find in their religious pursuits a coping mechanism, or an avenue for socialization, seem to have missed the point. Such people do exist. There is no question of a deliberate decision to pursue religion for self-serving purposes. Its roots lie perhaps in a painful lack of courage which needs an opiate. Nor can anyone of us claim immunity from such pain, or assert a chaste and selfless pursuit of true and godly religion. Motives are mixed and continuously call for purification.

Fortunately a purification of religious participation is underway, independent of our indolent selves. The world today can offer happy competition to religion narrowly conceived. Behavioral sciences and arts can give the individual person resources for coping, adjustment, and self-actualization. New lines of social organization and, even more impressively, communications technology can let people find and bind themselves as groups even as they retain a paradoxical but convenient anonymity. Obviously we cannot pour pure praise on the secular alternatives to meeting basic human needs once more generally met by religious life and institutions. The blessing is mixed and has, in fact, extorted a stipend in the form of a greedily consuming society, environmental damage, distorted political priorities, and psyches pushed and pinched by the latest movement. At times, the negative elements of secular alternatives lead people back to religion, especially of a more fundamentalistic caste. The overall pattern, however, seems to indicate that the secular alternatives will be around for a while. These alternatives, moreover, are forcing pastoral ministers and religious people to rethink their religious involvement.

If resources once offered by religious life and institutions are also available elsewhere, what precisely does religion have to offer? A response to that question involves returning to the "stories of paradise," returning to the village. Remember village life before the visit of the angels. Every need was met, every measure for happiness matched by the resources available and the harmonious lives lived there. Yet, when the messengers of the Lord appear and announce a favor from the Lord, no voices rise in response, "Thank you, but we're doing well enough now." As we hear the story, we naturally accept along with the villagers that paradise on earth gives way to paradise in heaven. What lies behind that instinctive reaching out for a heavenly offer? It is, I submit, a deeply rooted experience of the partial character of our lives. Even when our lives have every reason to stay contained within themselves, there is a hunger for fullness, an appetite that can be whetted but never satisfied.

The thought is very Augustinian. "Our hearts are restless until they rest in you." In light of this discussion, Augustine might elaborate our experience as a nostalgia for our origin and an anticipation of our glimpsed future. Our source, our origin is that life, is so full, so complete that it gives life. Our destiny is a fullness and a completeness that draws us forward each time we experience something, perhaps extraordinarily good, but always partial and therefore relative to a wholeness ahead.

The contented villagers reached out for the heavenly offer. Their representatives caught sight of the very fullness in heaven which motivated the villagers to accept the offer. But when the representatives returned to earth, they could only speak, as each one did, of the wholeness and the fullness in a partial way. The elder then took the partial descriptions, the several stories of paradise, and perceived in the silent waiting time perhaps not so much the unity of the stories as the people's desire for abundance.

The deeper longing, the hidden hunger, the desire beneath partial fulfillment by secular alternatives—these are all present. There is a movement of spirits. People involved in pastoral ministry can feel it. Surely, they have not seen the end of the stop-gap use of religion which fails to accept the joyous and, at times, fearsome responsibility of our creation in freedom. But beyond the stop-gaps, pastoral ministers can sense an urgent task for spiritual renewal that comes from the urgent and deep longings of the people they serve.

We began by noting two dimensions, both weighty and mobilizing, which speak of an urgent need for a renewal of spirituality. One is theological, the other is pastoral-formational. If these reflections on the stories of paradise, viewed theologically and pastorally, say anything, they underline the initial intuition. They urge us to do something and not to be stymied by the multiple claims of experience and method. More importantly, our reflections provide another intuition to break out of the many bewildering stories of paradise and equally numerous prescriptions for its construction. The concerns of theology and the concerns of pastoral formation point us in a direction of exploring spirituality. Both sets of concerns uncover the dual dimension of an approach to spirituality and spiritual renewal—study and formation.

The sort of thoughtful, patient reflection which the elder urged remains a task, more precisely, a theological study task, to be undertaken today. The need for pastoral-formational commitment runs parallel to the theological task. Like the villagers, we cannot and do not rest content merely with new insights into spirituality. For them as for us, there is a need for a commitment to a fuller appropriation of the transformation wrought in spiritual life. This stands clearly as a commitment to build and to accept, to do and to receive—always colored and shaped by the sense of our hunger for fullness. The stories of paradise also reflect an ideal interweaving of insight and commitment to change. Today, that ideal amounts to a mutuality and reciprocity of theological study and pastoral-formational life.

Where does this leave us? Have we even really settled on the stuff of study or basic areas of pastoral-formational life? Are we not toying with ideas and methods aprioristically, not knowing precisely the matter under discussion? These questions may stop us and confirm our suspicion that spirituality is mirage-like and vanishes as we approach it.

Once again, the opening stories of paradise provide an answer. Rather than running from the many different stories of paradise, the elder advises, "Let us listen again to these stories of paradise." In the intersection of experience, insight, and commitment occasioned by the stories, the villagers came to know and to begin to build. For us, the same pattern can emerge. Rather than fleeing from the many stories of spirit, let us listen to them and piece them together. Insight may follow. Ways of planning, building, renewing, and accepting may follow upon insight.

All this may appear vague and abstract. It is. Yet, the proposal is simple. Let us study the spiritual stories of people, listen deeply to their experience, and so search out and perhaps find threads that link them to each other, and them to us. Let us consider ways of pastoral formation that are attentive to the emerging and unfolding stories in the lives of our people, and so search out and perhaps find the loving power that works transformation. Concretely, the study proposed here is the study of spiritual autobiographies, written stories of faith experience. The formation to be explored later is spiritual direction as a ministry to the unwritten and often unspoken stories of faith today. The study of the past's stories implies a formation of stories today. Similarly, today's task of formation calls us to study other stories from another time but about a same experience.

The stage is set for our common endeavor. We know the urgency behind our reflections, some contemporary conditioning factors, and a possible avenue of approach.

At the end of the stories of paradise, we never do hear if the villagers succeeded in their task of building paradise on earth. Perhaps they are still building. That is, in any case, our current condition.

CHAPTER TWO

THE STUDY OF AUTOBIOGRAPHY

Stories of the Forest

Once there was a boy. He spent time with his grandmother. She had come to this country from a land far across the sea. When she spoke, words came out in halting English. Sometimes she relied on words from the old country to describe this or that. As she grew older, she loved to speak more and more about her homeland. She told her grandson about the forest that surrounded the town of her girlhood. He enjoyed her stories and listened with serious attention. When she spoke, she painted pictures that lived and moved. The forest in her stories moved with rapid intensity. The king and queen of the forest moved about on the quick flow of lights and shadows by day and moonbeams at night. The trees were loyal subjects who bowed and bent as their royal rulers passed among them. The birds of the forest formed a vast choir to entertain the royal couple. Occasionally, an evil prince would make war on the forest kingdom. With screaming thunder and powerful lightning bolts, he tried to conquer the forest. After a storm, one could see some of the valiant tree soldiers who had been felled in the battle. But try as he would, the evil prince never succeeded in conquering the forest kingdom. In fact, after his wars, life returned to the forest stronger and more vibrant and fresher than before. The little boy's imagination could barely keep pace with his grandmother's stories.

When the boy grew older, his grandmother died. He could no longer visit with her. Then came the day that he entered school and began to study with other children. In a science class, the teacher asked all the pupils to write a description of a forest. The boy had visited a forest many times and found it just as his grandmother had described it. He wrote some paragraphs about the forest kingdom, its king and queen, their peaceful reign, and the times they had to endure a war with an evil prince. When he stood up before the class with the seriousness of a seasoned and learned professor and read his paper aloud, he found much to his surprise that his classmates laughed and even his teacher smiled. But was this not the way the forest kingdom really was?

As the boy grew older, he became very proficient in science. Every once in a while, he wondered why his grandmother had filled his head with silly stories. But he could no longer ask her the question. She was gone. He continued his studies. His childish wonder about the forest ceded to his growing fascination with mathematical and chemical formulas which described the ecosystems of forests. He grew and felt fortunate that he had laid aside fantasy for fact, dreams for reality.

The boy grew into a man. He became the father of a son, the joy of his life. He spent time walking and talking with his young son. One warm summer day, they took a walk in the forest. Suddenly, a summer thunderstorm arose. They sought protection under a tree. His frightened son asked him, "What is this, Daddy?" "It is," he said, "the hot summer air colliding with a wave of cooler air. That makes the rain." "Then," his son replied, "they are fighting, and I'm afraid." The father wondered how his scientific explanation became a fable in the mouth of his son.

The Way of Stories

The stories of the forest reflect many experiences we have of studying and interpreting the world about us and the world within us. The immediate and striking fact of experience is the way we hear, learn, discard, re-learn, and often enough remain puzzled that the point of arrival circuitously leads us back in some way to the point of origin. Another perception may impress us along the road of study and interpretation. We never walk the road alone. We receive the stories of grandmother or of the scientists. No doubt we develop our own stories, but always in the interplay of what we have heard and what we experience. Still, an overall puzzling pattern surfaces in retrospect. The boy who goes to observe the forest after his grandmother's stories finds what he expected. The boy grown up as a man with a scientific viewpoint finds the ecosystems carefully described in scientific writings. The puzzle comes in wondering why grandmother told her stories, and why his son reverts to a personalized forest. Is there more than the current understanding, the up-to-date story? Is it all really a question of finding what we set out to find? In his questions, the man may wonder about his limited ability to know, to interpret, and to understand.

The condition of puzzlement is our own. How do we, or can we, move to understand and interpret the spiritual stories of others and so overcome the limited viewpoint circumscribed by our current knowledge and expectations? The question involves more than a quest for objectivity. The question touches on the removal of the interference we place between ourselves and the stories of others. If we want to hear the stories of others and study them and come to insight and commitment, how can we span the gap of different experiences? The question can be phrased in another way. How can we move beyond our own backlog of experience to tap into other experiences? Can we move beyond our present viewpoint? A particular value undergirds these questions. If we accept the stories of paradise, then we must acknowledge that sharing other experiences, and somehow unifying them, make possible a movement beyond our own partial perceptions and experiences on the way to the fulfillment of our deepest longings. The problem raised in the stories of the forest underlines the obstacles in such a movement. The pluralism of stories renders unity and coherence difficult. Further still, the apparent exclusivity of experience and interpretations in stories of the forest make unity and coherence virtually impossible to obtain. Perhaps we have landed in a fine philosophical stew. One way out is to examine theories of knowledge and perception; even the ultimate foundations and conditions of the possibility of knowledge which critically reveal our ability or inability to arrive at truth, meaning, and meaningfulness. Another, less abstract approach suggests itself. We can take specific instances of spiritual stories and learn how to hear them. We can bring questions which will cause us to stop and to take note, and not merely to presume our experience in the life of another person. It is this approach which we will shortly begin to develop. The end result ought to correspond to the task mentioned at the end of chapter one—to study the spiritual stories of people, listen deeply to their experience, and so search out and perhaps find threads that link them to each other, and them to us. To our reflections thus far in this chapter add one important caution. We cannot study these stories haphazardly. Otherwise, we find our experience projected on the screen of the lives of other people. We need critical-analytic tools for study.

The Study of Spirituality by Way of Autobiography

By now the reader knows the gist of the title of this section. Spirituality means not merely doing something "spiritual" or relying on pious invention. It is, at least in one important dimension, something studied. Furthermore, autobiographies provide a way of study by offering us an occasion to hear the stories of spirit and share in the experience of others.

Many autobiographies which recount the spiritual stories of people are available. We will focus on four people whose autobiographies provide appropriate material for a critical and analytical study of spiritual stories. They are Augustine, Teresa of Avila, Therese of Lisieux, and Thomas Merton. The reasons for their selection deserve some explanation.

All four people have a heightened experience of spiritual life. They have also exercised an influence on their own respective generations as well as subsequent generations. Their reception, then, signals a certain resonance within the larger community experience. That resonance is important, because a study of spirituality cannot rest content with an individualistic approach to Christian living. Spirituality must adequately reflect the individual and social, or ecclesial, dimensions of life in the Spirit. The personal stories of these individuals carry a weight whose measure excedes individual living. Their stories have an impact on a wider community. To study them or even, as we shall do, simply to use them as examples means that we are in touch with recognized and rich resources of Christian spirituality.

The four people selected represent a genuine crosscut of situations and conditions in which life in the Spirit is lived. For example, each one represents a different historical and cultural setting. For Augustine, this means fifth century North Africa and Italy; for Teresa of Avila, Spain of the sixteenth century; for Therese of

Lisieux, France of the nineteenth century; for Merton, Europe and
the United States in the twentieth century. Furthermore, the two
men and the two women capture that perennially distinctive, but
only recently re-appreciated, difference between living as a man
and living as a woman. Different life situations also mark the
selected authors. Both Teresa and Therese were women religious in
the Carmelite tradition. Augustine was an active bishop who confronted and ministered to the pastoral needs of his people. Merton
was the monk who left the world only to return in a different way
as its "contemplative critic."

The crosscut of experience in culture, history, sex, and life
situation generates a variety of spiritual stories, and strikingly different frames of expression. Rather than permitting us to impose
with ease a sameness of spirituality on the people we study, these
differences force us to reckon with a perduring and universal way of
"living gospel" life embodied in the most diverse forms. The unity
of Christian spirituality emerges, then, not from an artificial and
imposed set of categories but from the discovery of a deep-
rootedness in the gospel, and living by the Spirit. Eventually, this
dialectic of pluralistic forms and a unified, singly-rooted life will
bear significant implications for the formative dimension of spirituality. For now, a recognition of this situation deserves careful exploration in the study of spiritual stories.

In brief, we choose Augustine, Teresa, Therese, and Thomas
Merton, because their personal religious stories are significant, influential, broad in their community impact, and representative of
differences and sameness. In what follows, we shall not study them
in depth. Rather, we will note an approach or method that can
effectively and fruitfully be brought to bear on studying their autobiographies.

The Purpose and Results of Reading Autobiographies Critically

In the stories of the forest, the young boy automatically sees
the forest in figures pictured by his grandmother. When he grows
up and has a scientific education, he observes—again
automatically—the forest in scientific categories. Only at the end,
when his scientific categories confront his son's imaginative and

personalized portrayal of the storm, is he led to question and wonder about a purely scientific description and a personalizing, almost instinctive approach to the phenomena of the forest. A critical reading of autobiographies endeavors to provoke a similar confrontation of the reader's personal experience and the author's personal experience. In the difference between the two, the reader must stop and truly hear the other story, the other experience. The mode of provoking such a confrontation consists in bringing questions to the reading of the text. The questions highlight another's experience different than our own. We are stopped from easily imposing the categories of our own story, our own experience. Freed in some measure from the intrusion of our own experience, we can expand our vision by appropriating, at least in part, the other story.

Once we allow a number of people the possibility of speaking for themselves, once we appropriate a number of stories which articulate an experience different than our own, then we can search out patterns of relationship. We can link stories together and relate them to our own story. The unity of experience, however, emerges only after the uniqueness of individual experiences has gained proper recognition. This is no easy task. Our tendency runs in a certain direction. We learn, we discard, we review, we discard again, and learn again. At any given phase, we tend to canonize our current outlook. In stories of the forest, the man grown scientific could not hold the poetic-imaginative truth of the forest concomitantly with his scientific truth and, even less, sense some unity of vision in the two perspectives. The critical reading of autobiographies tries to overcome the difficulty of entrenchment in our own experience. If the reading succeeds, it opens up a world of multiple and unified experiences.

Several results flow from a critical reading of spiritual autobiographies. The first result is a set of generalized insights about spirituality; for example, how transformation takes place in the Christian life, how evil is confronted, what is the shape of our "communication" with God. These issues find ample treatment in manuals of spirituality but on an entirely different level. The manuals work deductively, proceeding from principle to specific instance. The study of autobiographies inductively yields insights concerning spirituality. The resultant picture of spirituality may be less rigorously systematic than the manualist's representation, but

it more likely mirrors the true life experience from which it origi-
nated. The first and extremely valuable result, then, of a critical
reading of spiritual autobiographies is an inductively constructed
sketch of Christian spirituality.

A second result regards a skill acquired in the process of reading spiritual autobiographies critically. Such reading provides a
practice laboratory. Attentive and critical reading of spiritual
stories develops the reader's skill in hearing and listening to the
story of oneself and others. Obviously, this result has significant
practical implications for formative spirituality, especially the art of
spiritual direction which will be discussed in a later chapter. For
now, it is sufficient to note the transferability of sharpening the
critical and analytical skills of reading autobiographies to the very
practical task of helping others in their spiritual journeys.

A third result of critically reading autobiographies also concerns a skill. Readers who come in contact with several people who
can skillfully unfold their life stories will find themselves equipped
to articulate their own spiritual stories, and those of others. We
learn to speak from those who already speak. Similarly, we learn
the vocabulary, the manner of selection and expression, the format
for telling a personal spiritual story from those who already have
done so.

The purpose and the results of reading autobiographies critically induce us to pursue the exact way in which such critical
reading is to be accomplished. The next task is to delineate some
questions which illustrate the critical approach.

General Questions for a Critical Reading

The two general questions mentioned in this section are
somewhat specific. The next chapter, on faith and story, will provide a wider, more general systematic base for making comparative
analyses and perceiving the unifying elements in the lives of very
different people. For now, the questions of this section and the
following one reflect a concern for approaching the individual texts
individually. The questions do not anticipate findings in the autobiographies. Rather, they enable the reader to pause and take the
story on its own terms. Two general questions begin our illustration of sample questions for a critical reading.

1. *What is our initial impression of the person whose autobiography is being read? What is our later impression?*

When we meet someone for the first time, we instinctively receive certain impressions. The impression may change later, but some "sizing-up" of the other person remains an important ingredient in the social management of our lives. From that impression, we will judge how seriously and deeply we will pay attention to the other person, how much we can permit ourselves to reveal who we are, what style of response we will employ in an exchange.

Obviously, the reciprocity of day to day meetings is absent in reading an autobiography. But, impressions are formed and determine our personal investment in hearing the other person's story. To be not only instinctively but also reflectively aware of these impressions contributes to a critical review of our reading process.

A reflective awareness of impressions also spells out the human context of personality, style, and traits in which the story unfolds. The sense of a human context can later provide a counterpoint for understanding particular developments or experiences. For example, Teresa of Avila may initially impress us as an especially introspective person. Reflecting on our impression and its origin, we recognize a woman who travels, founds convents, and reforms a religious order. But, she finds her true home in a restricted form of cloistered life which generates intense attentiveness to one's inner states. Later, her intricate and highly differentiated analysis of stages of prayer, from the perspective of the "soul's labor," fits the initial impression as coming from an introspective person. But the impression as reflected upon cautions us not to dismiss her analysis simply as the product of a certain personality type, and therefore limited in its applicability. She writes introspectively, because she lives in a context which favors reflective living. Certainly, her own personality enters the process. A reduction, however, of her approach to understanding prayer to a personality quirk misses the wider range of her reflection which develops in a specific context.

Finally, reflective attention to our initial, and later, impressions of the autobiographical authors reveals much about ourselves. By piecing together a number of impressions of a number of people, we can begin to ascertain our own biases. If we are consistently awestruck, or negative, or alienated, or "identifying with," the range of our own horizons becomes clear. If there are consistently identical patterns of impression emanating from different people, then our receptivity to others has pronounced limitations and needs expansion.

2. *Why did this person write an autobiography?*

Anyone who has attempted to do a résumé for a job application, or even attempted on a grander scale to write an autobiography, knows the difficulty of such a task. True exertion accompanies the organization and writing of one's life. Most of us succumb to inertia and never do it. But these people have done it. What, in their cases, is the energy and the force stronger than inertia? What is the deep human meaning which leads a person to make an autobiographical statement? Or, is there a strong religious impulse which initiates and sustains the arduous labor of autobiography?

In the instances of Teresa of Avila and Therese of Lisieux, external circumstances evidently played an important role. Teresa hesitantly took up the task of writing in response to her spiritual director's request. Therese also did so in obedience to her religious superiors. But external circumstances in the lives of these women, as well as for Augustine and Thomas Merton, yield to another movement and a deeper involvement. All of them write from a religious feeling of gratitude for the presence of God in the movement of their lives. The overall framework is a confession of praise and thanksgiving, as the title of Augustine's *Confessions* explicitly indicates, and as Therese of Lisieux notes on her first page in citing Psalm 88. She writes, ". . . . I'm going to be doing only one thing: I shall begin to sing what I must sing eternally: *The Mercies of the Lord*." (page 13) The confessional character of the autobiographies gives some general rationale for their composition. An even deeper and more highly personalized reason arises in seeing the autobiographical act as a specific and intense act of freedom.

To see autobiography as an act of freedom does not answer the original question, "Why did this person write an autobiography?" Each person's exercise of freedom deserves specific exploration. Situating the question in this perspective, however, opens a possibility for finding an answer in each case to the more general and certainly elusive question.

Karl Rahner has suggested that the moment of death is a moment in which we uniquely exercise our transcendental freedom. The moment of death patterned after Jesus' "Father, into your hands I commend my spirit" becomes the time of gathering a lifetime, affirming it and freely surrendering it into the Father's hands. At the precise moment when we confront the termination of this life, the supreme passivity of human life, we can gather our lives together and actively and freely say yes or no to who we have been, and where we now mysteriously find ourselves. It is the moment which calls for the freest and most trusting faith of a lifetime.

The autobiographical act anticipates the moment of death as the moment of transcendental freedom. The autobiographer draws together a life not at its end but in its process. Nonetheless, there is an ingathering, even if it is partial. Then within the framework of one's gathered personal story, the author can freely and religiously affirm the moments and movement of graced experience and negate the evil, the sin, and the lack of response to graced moments.

If autobiography represents in anticipatory fashion the supreme human and religious task of freely gathering and affirming and, at times, of negating the disparate elements of one's life, then our initial questions find a partial response. Why did this person write an autobiography? How was the force of inertia overcome? Is there a religious impulse at the heart of autobiography? The response refers to the act of freedom which animates the autobiography. But the response is partial, because it is general. It leads us to listen attentively to a specification of freedom in each autobiographical instance.

Specific Questions for a Critical Reading

A number of specific questions follow in this section. They continue to help us in a critical reading of the autobiographies. Again, the same four autobiographical instances of Augustine, Teresa, Therese, and Merton will serve as examples. The order of the questions does not imply a special logic or order of priority. One or another of the questions is important according to the stage of reading or retrospective reflection.

1. *Are there important words? What do they mean?*

Conversational language abounds with frequent catchwords. A slack-suited Midwestern tourist in Paris might stand before Notre Dame and pronounce it "a nice church." A teenager sees a new car speed by and declares that it is "cool." The words are frequent but really signify nothing but a "filler" for blank thought, or minimally involved reaction. Sometimes, however, a person's entire life direction, a person's spiritual life, can coalesce in a "big word" which at once symbolizes and energizes everything that person is about. So, for example, the evangelical life of Francis of Assisi takes shape around one word, "poverty." The history of Israel comes together in "covenant." In subtler fashion, the autobiographies contain "big words" which encapsulate a pivotal spiritual experience or stance. These words are evident either by their frequent employment or significant position. The reader can easily pass over them, unless there is a deliberate attentiveness to what the autobiographer is saying. Therese of Lisieux, for example, especially in the later sections of her autobiography speaks frequently of "love." At one point she writes, ". . . my *vocation*, at last I have found it. . . . MY VOCATION IS LOVE!" (page 194) The contemporary reader passes over the love-word as a commonplace which is currently devalued because of its frequent, facile, and equivocal use today. When "love," however, is situated in Therese's religious environment which was still tinged with the Jansenistic rigorous tradition when "love" is situated in her personal history of a struggle with scruples and the management of her perfectionistic bent, then the reader can share the fresh exuberance of her insight "My vocation is love!" The word now marks a profound event of self-transcendence. She has stepped beyond herself not in ecstatic experience but in entrance into a vaster vision of her life and her God. "Love" takes on an additional element of self-transcendence when linked to her sense of mission. She lives a restricted and enclosed life in the convent. Her possibilities for acting as a force for change in the world appear to be minimal. She is, as most would picture her, a powerless creature. When she experiences the gospel insight into the power of love, she transcends the ordinary categorizations of power or forces for change. She has appropriated the evangelical insight that power is not rooted in possibilities for domination but rather in a unitive and, ultimately, radically transformative love. She can then live an enclosed convent life limited in its extensive possibilities for affecting people and institutions but intensively open to her own and others' radical transformation. In contemporary terms, the quantity of life becomes subordinated to its quality.

These insights into Therese's spiritual story or experience are triggered by her use of the word "love." It is easy to glide over the word, not to listen to this moment of crystallization in her story. Attention to the important words in reading and listening is necessary for a critical reading or hearing of an individual's story.

2. *Is there a conversion-axis in the life of the person being read? How does it organize and interpret the life story?*

An awestruck youngster enters an ice cream shop with two dollar bills clutched in his hands. He stands ecstatically before the vast array of ice cream. He would like to consume the whole shop. He experiences one massive appetite for ice cream. Gradually, he perceives the different colors, the different flavors, the various combinations which are advertised. He has moved from being overwhelmed by the ice cream shop to an ability to make a final, if agonizing choice. The key to his ability to choose is his ability to perceive what is there. He begins to perceive what is there by the differences of flavor, color, and texture. Our ordinary capacity to perceive follows the same pattern. We perceive in an experience of difference and comparison.

The perception of ourselves and our life stories again follows the same pattern. We perceive ourselves in differences. The differences, however, are unlike the static qualities of the ice cream assortment. They are the changes which we make or undergo in our lives. Over a period of time, we can sight a number of changes, differences, which begin to permit us to form a picture of ourselves and our life stories. The sense of the question, "Is there a conversion-axis in the life of the person being read?" fits into this pattern of perception through differences and changes, but it bears further explanation.

The experience of conversion, taken in its general and not necessarily religious sense, is a complex experience. The person facing the autobiographical task explicitly or, more likely, implicitly grasps two interrelated personal experiences of the present moment. "I am not now what I once was." There is an experience of discontinuity in one's life. Yet that same person can say, "But I am now who I have been." There is an experience of continuity or flow in one's life. The autobiographer setting about the task of writing must account for the double experience of continuity and discontinuity. The writer may implicitly visualize a continuous line running through the middle of experiences, a line which represents a power and a force which induce and enable change, the discontinuous element. The double experience of continuity-discontinuity becomes organizationally and interpretatively present as a central continuous line inducing changes or discontinuity in the life story. Expressed in terms of the opening question, there is a conversion-axis about which life experiences are organized. This organizational and interpretative device matches the lived experience of continuity-discontinuity.

For people writing spiritual autobiography the axis implies more than a mental framework for literary expression. In reflecting upon and telling a life story, the central line of continuous change assumes its own characteristics. It touches me in a deeply personal manner and in bettering ways. So, it speaks of something more than myself, drawing me beyond who I am now and where I stand. It generates a coherent and intelligible unfolding of many disparate events and relationships. The conversion-axis points to a personal, good, and wise presence which is more than myself and not myself yet inextricably intertwined with my deepest areas of life. Spiritual autobiographers speak of a personal providence or an experience of God which unfolds in their telling of their life stories perceived through a series of continuous changes.

How does looking for a conversion-axis which may not even explicitly appear in an autobiography contribute to the critical reading of a life story or to our personal appropriation of the story and the experience of another person? An example may help us to answer the question.

It is possible to read Thomas Merton's autobiography and to grasp factually the changes in his life. He experienced two major changes or conversions, his religious conversion to Roman Catholicism and his entrance into monastic life. He also experienced a number of lesser changes. Having read his story in this way, we have grasped a chronology in his life and have appropriated information about him. In other words, we have come to know biographical data about him. But we have not appropriated his story nor his experiences until we enter his process which is beyond the collection of informational data. Autobiography, in contrast to biography, invites us to enter the sphere of Merton's organizing and interpreting the events of his life story, the way he perceives himself through change and sameness, through continuity and discontinuity. It is, then, not simply a question of talking about or hearing about the past. The talk about the past occasions the present autobiographical event which discloses his experience of God in the continuity-discontinuity of his life. That is what Merton's autobiography beckons us to share in. But we only participate in the autobiographical experience on the condition of reflectively organizing and interpreting his life along with him according to the "axis" which he perceives running through his life.

An illustration from Merton's autobiography may serve to clarify the discussion of conversion-axis. Merton portrays himself as a man who is sensitive to artistry and beauty in life. He traces his aesthetic sensitivity to his father who was an artist. As Merton describes the movement of his life, he consciously portrays the continuous flow of a sense of the beautiful. It is that very flow which draws him into a number of changes. First, for example, when he is a young man traveling about Europe, he experiences a mysterious attraction to the churches and monuments of European Catholicism. An aesthetic appreciation leads him to visit and study these places. As he grows older, the experience of the attractive and beautiful power of Catholic liturgy pulls him even closer to Catholicism and eventually contributes in some measure to his Roman Catholic conversion. After his conversion, a continuous attraction to the contemplation of the presence of God in solitude, in nature, in the lives of good people—all experiences of the beautiful— contribute to his movement into the Trappist monastery of Gethsemani. He vividly portrays the monastic life in a series of tableaux, the community of monks set in a stark and simple background in a way reminiscent of the spare lines of modern art. He recognizes and affirms his own monastic vocation at the end of *The Seven Storey Mountain* as a calling to contemplation; the contemplation of prayer no doubt but also and more determinately of a vision of the beautiful one who has drawn him to this point. Sharing in the conversion-axis which belongs to Merton the autobiographer, we enter into Merton's autobiographical experience. We have moved beyond the simple acquisition of information about him and his life into the realm of his deep experience of self.

3. *What are the correlations of inner and outer life? What are the relationships between interiority and external circumstances?*

A reader approaching spiritual autobiography ordinarily has a definite interest in the autobiographer's interiority or, experience of self and God and the two in relationship. Outer circumstances of life, although they may claim some interest, appear to be secondary to the inner story of the person. Outer circumstances, then, merely function instrumentally in providing a backdrop for the heart of the matter.

In fact, this is not so. There is a real, important, and intimately related connection between inner and outer life. Take, for example, the life of a workingman on Chicago's Southside. What he does, the hours of work, how he attends to his house, the time spent with his family—all these fall in the range of outer circumstance. At the same time, however, the outer circumstances reveal a number of inner commitments, to productivity, to an ordered life, to a stable and securely provided for family. Interestingly, although now his inner commitments guide and shape his outer experience, at one time it may have been the other way around. As a young unmarried man, he entered the work force; and an entire set of outer circumstances in the form of fellow workers and paychecks and the discipline of company demands triggered a repositioning of what he wanted in life and how he would commit himself.

The illustration indicates general correlations between inner and outer life. Outer experiences can reveal something about interiority, which, of course, in its entirety remains opaque. Correlatively, interiority manifests itself in outer experiences, although the dynamism of inner life may outpace the capacity to embody it in one's outer circumstances. The illustration also indicates another correlation. Outer life can not only manifest inner life, it can also give rise to and shape interiority. Correlatively, inner life not only manifests itself in outer experiences but can also creatively determine and shape those experiences. Finally, notice both in the illustration and the analysis of the illustration that the correspondence between inner and outer experience on either level mentioned above is always partial, never perfectly adequate. A tension results on the levels of manifestation and determination. The tension sustains a movement in which inner and outer experience attempt to "catch up" with each other.

The attentive reader of spiritual autobiographies brings the question of correlating inner and outer experience to the reading. Although the question has general value for reading any autobiography, it plays an especially important role in the reading of Christian spiritual autobiography because of the decisively historical character of Christian religion. An elaboration of this point will serve to clarify the question from another perspective and to help specify our reading task.

Christianity is an historical religion in the sense that it traces its roots to the revelation or self-disclosure of God in history. The decisive moment of this revelation in history is, of course, Jesus Christ. Christianity is an historical religion in a somewhat different sense. The authentically lived Christian experience represents a continuous intertwining of individuals' and communities' events and a corresponding interpretation, understanding, and appropriation of those events in faith. The Catholic tradition, in its wide sense of sacramentality, gives striking witness to the historical character of Christian religion. The Christian religious experience cannot be isolated simply in external life events, nor simply in a set of inner dispositions. Birth, marriage, reconciliation, community mission and order do not stand by themselves, nor do faith, hope, or love. The event of birth, for example, finds its inner meaning in the ritual of baptism as a rebirth into a new life of faith, which brings new hope for a destiny of loving communion with others and with God. In short, the external, historical event is intertwined with its inner meaning in faith. When periods or movements within Christian history have tended to emphasize exclusively either the inner or the outer dimension of Christian life, inevitably a weakened and inadequate form of Christianity has resulted. Movements of "inner Christianity" which underline in exclusive fashion thought, interpretation, or inner feeling generate a partial Christianity which is intellectualist or sentimental. Movements of "outer Christianity" which highlight in an exclusive way patterns of behavior, automatic ritual, or external ecclesiastical affiliation produce a partial Christianity which is moralistic or lopsidedly institutional.

This broad analysis of Christianity as an historical religion has implications for the study of the personal history of Christian believers. Their individual lives will mirror the intertwining of inner and outer experience. The question, then, of reading spiritual autobiographies with an eye on the correlation of inner and outer experience is not simply based on a general philosophical datum of life. The question arises from the very character and quality of Christian faith.

A sample analysis of Augustine's life can give some idea of the reflection which follows from attentiveness to the correlation of inner and outer experience. Augustine presents a series of external geographical movements in the *Confessions*. His major movements are from Africa, to Rome, to Milan. There are other movements involving lesser distances. Augustine also presents a series of inner movements of intellectual and personal commitment. He moves from the study and teaching of rhetoric, to the discovery of philosophy, to involvement with the dualistic sect of the Manichees, and, finally, to the Christian faith. Again, on the internal level there are other movements which involve less change. Now, although the geographical moves do not match his movements of inner commitment exactly, there is a general correlation. The movement from place to place reveals a searching, a physical restlessness which corresponds to the restlessness of his heart. At the same time, his movement from place to place draws him into encounters which challenge him, force him to revise his positions, at times disappoint him and leave him empty, and, ultimately, engage him totally.

A reader of the *Confessions* could easily bypass a fuller appropriation of Augustine's experience by seeing two tracks in the autobiography. There is a set of external circumstances or outer experiences. Then, there is the real material of the *Confessions*, Augustine's inner journey. It is quite obvious that such an approach misses a fuller entrance into his story.

The point is clear. A critical reading of autobiography, especially spiritual autobiography, incorporates the question of correlating inner and outer experience.

4. *What are the striking notes of cultural dissonance? Which expres-*

*sions are, and remain, alien and alienating? Do the strange elements speak
of a deeper unity with contemporary experience?*

After I had been in Italy for a while and knew the language
well, I was surprised by my lack of assimilation the first time I
stayed with an Italian family for several weeks. I thought that
knowing the language and doing the work of mental translation
from Italian into English was enough to build communication
bridges. I had not counted on the existence of another unspoken
and unwritten language. It was the nonverbal language of psychological cues, of expressing feelings, of reacting and responding to
others. I knew the spoken language, I even knew the family somewhat before coming to live with them. But now I felt a sense of
alienation, an experience of being a stranger. That experience
emerged each time I confronted a cultural dissonance, a way or a
manner that failed to match the expectations of my cultural background. How did I deal with those dissonances? The way most
people do with a certain flight into cultural imperialism. I could
write off the difference as idiosyncratic. "That belongs to the Italian temperament. It certainly isn't the way Americans do things."
As long as I kept that posture, there was little possibility of sharing
the life experiences of that good family. When I confronted the
strangeness instead of writing it off, then I began to perceive a
deeper communality of human experience which could cross bor-
ders back and forth rather freely. Differences surely remained, but
they became enriching rather than alienating. I began to share in
the family's life.

The reading of autobiographies written in cultural settings
different from our own can jolt us with striking cultural dissonances. This experience alienates us and distances us from the
experience of the autobiographer. The very purpose of reading and
studying autobiography is undercut. Instead of coming to a fuller
appropriation of another's story, we find ourselves critiquing the
experience and disassociating ourselves from it. Such a massive
obstacle needs removal. Otherwise our reading leaves us confirmed
and stagnated in our own perspective. No differences, appropriated
or even understood, mean quite simply that we have changed in no
way.

To confront cultural dissonances and the experience of alienation requires attention on two levels, the hermeneutical and the
participatory. The work of hermeneutics, as Bible scholars and

theologians have abundantly indicated, involves establishing the principles of interpretation. The hermeneutical task includes more than a translation from language to language. It also demands a more arduous labor of cultural translation. Just as the personal experience of living in Italy showed me the inadequacy of simple linguistic ability, so the process of interpretation must move beyond language to examine and establish the total context in which something was composed and make meaningful interpretations which speak to our contemporary cultural situation. For the Bible and other religious writing a foundational theological principle is at stake. God's movement in history does not manifest itself in utterances of universally valid abstractions. Rather, God's movement takes life and shape in particular cultures and people and frameworks. So, the first level of dealing with cultural dissonances encountered in spiritual autobiography is hermeneutical, the level of searching out the context in culture and attempting to match that cultural experience with dimensions of our own.

The second level of working with cultural dissonances in autobiographies is participatory. The Bible scholar fulfills the demands of hermeneutics by interpreting the biblical text not only linguistically but also culturally. The preacher has the additional task of taking the interpreted text and facilitating its appropriation, so that people can participate in it today. Similarly, in reading spiritual autobiographies the interpretation of cultural dissonance in ways that eliminate or reduce the dissonance and facilitate cross-cultural understanding is a fundamental and important task. In effect it means drawing another's experience into the framework of my own experience. This movement, however, does not take full account of the purpose of reading the spiritual autobiographies, which is entering into and participating in the experience and story of another. This is the participatory question in confronting cultural dissonance. It means moving in the other direction, from my experience to the writer's experience, even when the author's experience appears to be alien and alienating. A theological understanding explains both the rationale and the method of this movement.

The "Christian experience" does not exist as an independent entity in a world of ideal forms. The Christian experience takes flesh and blood in the lives of individual Christians and the communities they form. This pattern of Christian experience, or experiences, implies particularity and diversity in concrete living. Any single Christian or group of Christians will reflect a partial and proper way of living Christian life. What links these individual and particular experiences is their rootedness in Jesus Christ who is the universal normative pattern and the creative full resource for the various possibilities of Christian experience. Any number of references from the Bible could be cited to substantiate this awareness. One particularly forceful statement is found in Paul's letter to the Galatians (3:26–28): "Each one of you is a son of God because of your faith in Christ Jesus. All of you who have been baptized into Christ have clothed yourselves with him. There does not exist among you Jew or Greek, slave or freeman, male or female. All are one in Christ Jesus." In effect, the passage and others like it note deep differences among those who believe but subordinate (and in Paul's style even obliterate) difference to the radical unity of experience in Christ. Applied to the dissonances and differences of autobiographical statements, this insight means that such differences are transcended when the other's experience is referred to its origin in Christ. Indeed, by taking the difference and tracing it to its origin, the reader gains insight into the radical communality of experience underlying differences and is able to participate and share in the different experiences in reference to the full and universally valid base of experience in Christ. In this way, the reader comes not only to grasp the autobiographer's experience in terms of the reader's experience (hermeneutical level) but also comes to share in the autobiographer's experience in terms of the autobiographer's and reader's mutually rooted experience of Christ (participatory level). This highly theoretical discussion needs concrete examples to specify what is meant.

In addressing God, Teresa of Avila often uses the form "Your Majesty." A current American pattern of the rhetoric of prayer opts for a more familiar form and says "Father" or "Heavenly Father," or "Loving Father." In reading Teresa as contemporary Americans, we sense a certain jarring of our sensibilities. There is a dissonance with our own way of praying. One possible reaction is to evaluate her form as "old fashioned" or "dated" and then to move on in search of elements that do resonate with our experience. A critical reading, as we have noted earlier, cannot be content with the tactics of evasion. The difference demands confrontation.

An initial confrontation on the level of cultural interpretation seeks to locate Teresa's phrase "Your Majesty" in its cultural and historical framework. In this interpretative reflection, we discover a reason and a meaning behind her usage. Teresa belongs to sixteenth century Spain ruled by powerful kings and queens. Clearly, then, Teresa is employing the courtly form of address to God. In doing so, she takes the national experience of power and dominion and applies it to her experience of God as powerful and sovereign. With the cultural-historical context in mind, we can translate her form of address as reflective of our contemporary naming of God as "infinite mystery," "ground of being," or another title which evokes for us a sense of God's power. Although our own cultural bent is more personalistic and familiar, there are elements of our experience which resonate with Teresa's, but beneath the verbal expression, on the level of meaning. At this point, we have a translation or interpretation of Teresa's experience in terms of our own. The next task involves sharing or participating in her experience on the basis of our common rootedness in the experience of Christ. By utilizing the experience of Christ considered in the sense of the experience of Jesus himself as portrayed in the gospels, and the experience of Jesus by the early community, also portrayed in the gospels, we can coordinate and share in what Teresa writes with our own contemporary experience.

A reading of the gospels indicates Jesus' experience of the Father was both intimate and familiar. He also experienced the Father as the powerful source of his own mission. Manifestations of his closeness to the Father were so striking as to be taken for blasphemy. His supreme confidence in his mission and his work which was not supported by ordinary human, institutional, political, monetary, or ideological resources, speaks of a transcendently all powerful God, capable of creation and transformation. The early community speaks of its experience of the Spirit of Jesus in a similar way, as intimately situated in their hearts yet powerfully present in spreading the message. The intersection of power and intimacy in the biblical witness corresponds to the double experience of "Your Majesty" and "Loving Father," the double experience of Teresa and ourselves confronted when we read her autobiography today. When our differently shaped experiences meet in their common origin, we are enabled to understand Teresa and, more importantly, share in her experience.

5. *What developments in the autobiography reveal the immanence and transcendence of grace?*

Truly significant human relationships have a life of their own. They represent something more than the sum of their parts. A marriage which is really working, for example, is more than the combined contributions of man and wife. Both spouses live in a sphere greater than themselves as two individuals, a sphere which also affects and changes them as individual persons. The stories of spiritual experience in autobiographies represent a relationship of the individual with God. The discernible side of that relationship for us is the life of the human person. It soon becomes evident in hearing that person's story that there is an element of identity, "I remain myself," along with a personal sense of non-identity, "I am becoming more than myself." These phrases express the experience of the self-transcending person drawn in relationship with transcendence itself. The relationship, at least from the human side, bears more than the marks of human self-betterment. Yet, throughout the process, the human person remains the same human person, and change occurs precisely in terms of that personal identity. Another way of expressing the same phenomenon employs the theological terms of the "immanence and transcendence of grace." In brief, these terms reflect the bidimensional experience of the spiritual person in relationship to God: a sense of being oneself in the relationship and also becoming more than oneself because of the relationship.

The rationale for the bidimensional character of religious experience emerges in response to a question. What are the conditions for a finite creature to have access to the infinite creator? Or, expressed more concisely and simply, what is the way to God? Reflection on the terms of the question corroborated by the biblical experience yields a double answer; the way to God is God. The finite cannot build a road to the infinite. Anything that is of our construction remains a product of the finite and finite itself, hardly capable of leading into the infinite source of all creativity. To say that the way to God is God means that God alone must give us access to God's life, if we are to have access. But, surprisingly this is only half of the answer to the question. It is *we*, finite human beings, who seek a way to God. If this is so, then the way must be one that we can traverse. It must be a human way. To say that the way to God must be a human way means that the human pilgrims must be on a road which they can travel as human beings. What is the way to God? Paradoxically, we respond that it must be God giving and given to us; at the same time, the gift must be within the reach of human beings to receive it.

The question about the way to God and the double response are at the heart of the basic issues of Christology, its formulations and understandings. The Christian faith professes that Jesus Christ is the one way to the Father, our unique access to God. The mystery of his existence is that he personally synthesizes the double response—the divine and the human, the infinite and the finite, the transcendent and the immanent. Beyond Christology, the same mysterious synthesis operates in the lives of believers.

The spiritual stories of autobiography develop a life of relationship with God. Within that relationship people experience themselves as themselves, and themselves as transformatively gifted, going beyond themselves. The giftedness unfolds *in* the life story of the individual. So, whatever the transformative effects of being in relationship to transcendence are, they unfold within the individual's life, immanently or humanly. There is a synthesis of immanence and transcendence. This synthesis provides a conceptual framework for understanding the dynamics of the autobiographer's unfolding relationship with God, recounted in the autobiography. A critical reading with the perspective of the immanence and transcendence of the way to God allows us to enter into the life dynamics of the person being read.

How does the perspective of the immanence and transcendence of grace concretely affect our reading of autobiography? The instance of Therese of Lisieux provides an example. The immanent or human dimension means careful attention to the details of life, personality pattern, conditioning environment, and all the other factors which affect the unique configuration of this human being. The employment of psychological studies, contextualizing historical studies, and any other tools which analyze human behavior and development can be helpful in focusing on the immanent or human development of the person.

In Therese's life, we find a background at home and in the convent, a set of family conditions, and an environment in provincial France in the last quarter of the nineteenth century—all of which contribute to her development as a self-conscious person whose awareness spans a narrow range.

At the end of her life, Therese has moved well beyond a self-conscious posture. She directs her attention to others. She experiences an ever expanding sense of love. Finally, she becomes aware in some mysterious way of a call to a mission which goes beyond her death and beyond the people with whom she has had immediate contact.

Between narrowness and expansion, a process of transformation has taken place. Precisely in those areas of her life which read so heavily of narrowness, she grows into a person of expansive vision. She is gifted beyond herself.

In this brief and partial reflection on Therese's life, the immanence and transcendence of grace, the human element and the transformative effects of her relationship with God, become evident. The analysis implied by the opening question provides another important way of critically reading the autobiographies, not merely for information but as a way of entering deeply and appropriating personally the spiritual stories of others.

6. *What is the shifting style of prayer evident in the autobiography, a style which reflects a shifting image of God for the autobiographer?*

When a boy meets a girl, they form an impression of each other. The impression generates an image of each other, or, in other words, who this boy or this girl is for me. The image of the other person remains my inner possession and is therefore inaccessible in a direct way. There is, however, indirect access to the person and the inner image of the other person; who that person is for me. The form of address, the style of dialog or exchange, mirror the image of the other person. So, for example, the initial exchanges between the boy and the girl may be stiff and stilted. They carry inner images of each other of awe, a kind of distant, and perhaps even fearful, admiration for each other. This style changes, and they begin to exchange chatty information about what they like, their families and personal history. The image has changed. They exercise a powerful fascination on each other. They want to know each other. One day, perhaps hesitantly they begin to express their feelings for each other, their mutually positive regard, their affection. The boy and girl now image each other as lovable, as people who share the possibility of closeness. Eventually, if the relationship grows, they declare to each other their mutual love. They have decisively shifted their image of each other. No longer do they simply represent persons with whom particular experiences can be shared. Now, they represent for each other partners who can share life in its full span. The development of their shared life finds them speaking fewer words, simply being present to each other in nonverbal ways for longer periods of time. In effect, this final "form of dialog" represents the fusion of their image of each other into a shared identity.

The example of the boy and girl in a growing relationship has many parallels with the growing relationship with God present in spiritual autobiographies. The exact image of God, who God represents for the person, has an indirect accessibility. One way of noting the relationship as an experience of God, and seeing that relationship as a growing or dynamic one, is to examine attentively and reflectively the shifting style of prayer which the autobiographer presents. The form of approach to God, the style of dialog, can reveal in some measure what is an ineffable and indescribable experience which encompasses the whole person. The question of the form of prayer contributes to the critical reading of the autobiography and eventually to the personal appropriation of the autobiographer's story.

Therese of Lisieux once again provides an example of how this question can be pursued. The following analysis which is brief and partial is a sample. Anyone who reads her *Story of a Soul* will also note that there is overlapping in the stages of prayer which parallel her stages of a developing relationship with God. Overlapping is predictable, because the lived experience outpaces its analysis.

When Therese is a youngster, she presents a number of particular petitions to God. They are requests for favors. She makes little offerings to God. Her image of God at this stage is very much assimilated to her father. Just as her father who calls Therese "my little queen" gives her gifts of kisses and special treats, so too, Therese's heavenly Father supplies her with particular favors in return for her requests. God for her is the one who gives. As a young religious in the convent, Therese becomes remarkably involved in the meditative reading of Sacred Scripture. The abundance of biblical citations in her autobiography indicates her close contact with the Bible. The God of this time of her life has become the one who discloses Himself, the God who willingly and freely communicates Himself through the pages of Scripture which recount His ways and attitudes. Therese, the autobiographer, addresses God, as we noted earlier, in praise and thanksgiving "singing the mercies of the Lord." An image of God which has been germinal before, now flowers in her writing. God is the lovable one who loves her and takes her as His bride. Notice how the shifting forms of address to God manifest a shifting image which corresponds to her developing relationship. The last year of her life brings this movement into a range of dramatic intensity which deserves particular consideration.

For the last year of her life up to the very moment of her death, a powerful darkness overtakes Therese. She wonders whether or not she really is a believer. She suffers temptations to her faith. She experiences a paradoxical combination of deep anguish in her feelings of the absence of God and, at the same time, a deeper sense of peaceful joy. Her prayer at this time is marked by silence in an attitude of total surrender to God. A number of interpretations of her dark night are possible. In light of her previous development and movement, one particular interpretation seems to match her experience. Her prayer points to a relationship with God which becomes more and more intimate and tending toward union. As she approaches union, her symbolic universe, a world of faith and biblical and previously developed images, collapses. For, symbol, in etymology and in fact, represents a reality which "throws together" (*sym-ballein*) or holds together two realities. If the two realities are to be intimately united, then even symbols which have bridged the relationship must give way and fall apart, so that the distance between the two can be overcome. At the end of her life, Therese experiences the further movement into union with God. Her utterly free and simple prayer of surrender gives witness to this. The union, however, occurs in the measure that even her previously good and valid mediations of the relationship with, and the experience of God, give way to a possibility of a more immediate union. Her experience of the absence of God and faith speak of the death of the images of earlier times which now stand in the way of a new possibility for union.

This analysis of Therese's development highlights the significance of the question of this section "What is the shifting style of prayer evident in the autobiography, a style which reflects a shifting image of God for the autobiographer?" It should be clear that a response to this question enables us to enter into the spiritual autobiographer's dynamics of development in the relationship with God.

7. How does the autobiographer select out certain events or issues for the purpose of writing autobiography? What do the autobiographer's choices reveal about decisive moments of spiritual experience?

Reporting a story always involves making choices about what to include and what to leave unsaid. Ordinarily the principle or principles of selection are left unsaid or implicit. But when the reader consciously appreciates why certain elements are included and others not, then the reader can appreciate the story behind the story, the meaning behind the reporting. Compare, for example, journalistic reporting and autobiographical writing. Both deal with events. The journalist cannot include every item involved in a bank robbery. A selection of items needs to be made ordinarily on the basis of the readership's interest. If the readers belong to groups of professionals involved in finance, the newspaper story will highlight the economic consequences of the robbery. If the readers are more oriented toward human interest and action topics, the article will no doubt include a vivid reconstruction of the crime and its effect on people in the bank. Awareness of the journalistic principles of selection help the reader to interpret and understand by recognizing what is covered, what is not, and why.

Writers of spiritual autobiography also select out certain events and issues for insertion and reflection. They choose for many reasons, and one, like journalism, may be the intended readership. Merton, for example, wants to give witness to his story and so strike some sympathetic vibrations among his contemporaries who may be involved in a similar religious journey. Teresa of Avila writes for her spiritual director. But besides an intended readership, spiritual autobiographers also have another more decisive principle for choosing certain events and issues.

Spiritual autobiographers construct a continuous narrative of their lives and experience of God. They mark out the continuous flow of development, as we noted in the instance of Therese of Lisieux's life of prayer. They also note specific events and issues which represent pivotal moments or turning points or break-throughs in their lives. These moments represent what the au-tobiographers perceive as *kairoi*, the graced times when develop-ment comes to a focus and the invitation to change becomes a compelling reality. Retrospectively, these moments represent key-stones in the construction and development of one's life story.

The question of attentively noting these decisive life moments is in one sense a simple task for the reader of autobiography. Often the moments are transparently evident simply by the stylistic pre-sentation of the author. A difficulty arises, however, when the deci-sive moments, events, or issues are not so clearly evident, when in fact they appear intially as oddly exaggerated, out of place, or even trivial. Then the reader may simply bypass certain events without noting their critical importance for a full picture of the person's story.

Augustine, for example, writes many pages about an incident which took place when he was about sixteen years old. He de-scribes how he with a group of contemporaries stole pears. He dwells on the evil of their action. He describes its maliciousness. They stole the pears not to eat them but simply to do something evil. Eventually, they threw the pears to pigs. He describes how for a time the band of boys had formed a community of evil with each member inciting the others and supporting them in their activity. Augustine's reaction in the *Confessions* is shame and horror at what he had done. The reader's reaction may be astonishment at the length of time devoted to this youthful prank, and hesitancy in devoting much time for reflection on Augustine's experience.

A more reflective reading of the incident reveals how the pear tree story takes on pivotal significance for Augustine. He struggles throughout his life to deal with the problem of evil, not as an abstract question but in terms of the evil of his own life. This explains his attraction to the Manicheans with their facile and ulti-mately inadequate explanation of evil in a metaphysical dualism. A major breakthrough on the way to conversion occurs when he comes to claim ownership of his evil, when he recognizes his re-sponsibility. It is no longer the fault of friends or environment or an outside principle of darkness. It is Augustine who freely carries the burden and the consequences of sin. Retrospectively, the pear tree incident becomes a reassimilation of an earlier event in light of his later conversion. He relives in the retelling the personal experience of his freely chosen evil action. In so doing he claims responsibility for himself and can, in a stance of confessing his sin, be open to the forgiveness he seeks from God. The relatively minor significance of stealing pears only highlights in contrast his self caught up in and catching up with a personal dynamism of evil. Read in this way with attention to Augustine the converted one returning to his life events and selecting decisive moments, the pear tree incident reveals not only an event but the story behind the reporting of the event.

The questions cited at the beginning of this section are important. How does the autobiographer select out certain events or issues for the purpose of writing autobiography? What do the autobiographer's choices reveal about decisive moments of spiritual experience? They lead us to a critical reading of the text and a personal appropriation of the author's story by insisting that we return to understand the writer's own critical principles of selection and inclusion. In this way, we can come again to that important point of receiving the story and the experience on the writer's terms not simply on our own terms.

8. *What are the significant human relationships which both mirror and evoke the autobiographer's history of the experience of God?*

The style and quality of human relationships and interactions demanded by the gospel easily admit misunderstanding and reductionism. The human interaction of which the gospel speaks does not simply represent, as some would have it, a set of moral or ethical consequences. Nor does such interaction simply reflect a deeper reality at work in the soul. The gospels are more daringly direct than we would be. The gospels, and the witness of the Bible in general, present human interaction as an area of the experience of God. The Spirit of God, according to the New Testament, works not only in the hearts of believers but is the active bond of unity among them. The sphere of connection between people in relationship and interaction is an area of the experience of God. From a somewhat different and more dynamic perspective, we can arrive at the same conclusion. Significant human interpersonal experiences affect us deeply by evoking new possibilities and pulling us beyond the confines of our own self constructions. Such experiences open us in new and transformative ways to new love, a new vision of the world, and wider ranges for our personal contribution to the world. When we experience creative transformation drawing us forward in a movement of self-transcendence, we experience the movement of God in our lives, who is the source of creative force drawing everything into a future fullness. A number of theological presuppositions underlie these statements. They cannot be developed here. Their conclusion, however, and an example may clarify what they mean.

The conclusion is simple. If human interpersonal relationships and interactions represent the unifying work of the Spirit and if, furthermore, such relationships and interactions make dynamically present the creative, transformative, and future-oriented movement of God in our lives, then reflective attention to these relationships will give us entrance into a way in which we experience God and how that experience develops. Reflection on the well known parable of the Good Samaritan in Luke's gospel may help us to understand this conclusion.

A quick and easy way for a contemporary preacher to make the Good Samaritan "come alive" today might involve the reconstruction of the parable in modern terms. An unfortunate black traveler falls into the hands of a vicious gang while driving on an interstate highway. He is left half dead. A doctor, a civic leader, and a priest pass by the scene. A white power proponent known for his racist views comes by, stops, and takes care of the black victim. The preacher concludes by exhorting his congregation to be ready to help anyone in need, even those who are much different than ourselves. In this way, we fulfill God's commandment to love our neighbor. The preacher has not preached falsely. He certainly gives good advice to his congregation. But has he captured the full meaning of the parable by highlighting its moral application? He has not, it seems. A fuller exposition of the parable ought to include an examination of the significant human interaction between the Samaritan and the victim and how the interaction reveals an encounter with God.

The context of the story is human debris, a victim of violence stripped, beaten, and laid aside. Within that ugly context, an unlikely helper, unlikely because he belongs to a different and racially antagonistic group, appears on the scene. The help he renders the victim represents a new and unexpected response, as well as his own movement out of expected and predictable categories. Instead of rejection, there is acceptance; instead of bypassing, a confrontation with the situation; instead of indifference, compassion; instead of minimal attention, abundant care. In the novelty and unexpectedness of the encounter, the Samaritan is drawn beyond himself. He experiences and embodies God-love, the unconditionally accepting, confrontative, compassionate, and abundant love that is so powerful that it "sees through" the debris of the human situation. The God experience in this human interaction emerges in the bond between the two men, a bond that is more than something of their own making, and in the creative transformation which is more than the product of circumstance.

For the reading of spiritual autobiography, the conclusions regarding human relationships and encounters alert us to be attentive to the author's portrayal of significant relationships and encounters. They are more than influences or reflections of deeper realities. They embody an experience of God and the development of that experience. The reflections on the Good Samaritan further indicate that attentive reading of these relationships and encounters requires locating their binding power and creative-transformative effects. A study of Thomas Merton's relationship with his brother, John Paul, gives an example of reading with critical attention to significant relationships.

John Paul does not appear frequently in Merton's *Seven Storey Mountain*, but he does appear regularly throughout the story of Merton's life. Merton's perception of John Paul at various ages keeps shifting. Merton's changing perception, in turn, reveals a changing bond between the two brothers as well as the transformative impact of the relationship on Merton's life.

When John Paul is a baby, his smiling joyful face represents for the young Merton a basic goodness and innocence in the world. He relates to his brother with playful delight and fascination with new life in the world. A scene from his later boyhood is emblazoned in Merton's memory. Merton, the older brother, excludes John Paul from his circle of playmates, and John Paul stands across the way alone and alienated. The bittersweet memory of the distance across the yard signifies for Merton, in the language of maturity, an initial intimation of the alienation and the rejection of sin. The gap in the relationship convicts Merton of his possibility for personal evil. Much later, John Paul, the would-be college student at Cornell who takes a battered jalopy around the country, relates to Merton as a free and instinctual spirit in sharp contrast to Merton himself, who is also free in his life and pursuits but because of a paradoxical drivenness and nervous experimentation in trying to find himself. His relationship to John Paul seems to contribute to Merton's new and transformative process of simply listening to himself. Later, when Merton has entered the monastery and become a novice, John Paul comes to visit him and to be received into the Catholic Church. Flesh brothers come to share in the same spirit, but in remarkably different ways which force Merton to reassess his own style. Merton comes into the Church on the wings of the Catholic philosophical, theological, and aesthetic traditions. He moves with questions, he searches for solutions, and he makes endless critical reflections. John Paul enters the Church simply, with a basic trust and desire. He does not even own the basics of religious information which Merton attempts to supply in a few short frantic days before John Paul must leave for an RAF assignment in Europe. The questioning intellectual confronts simple trust and love and is changed by it. Finally, John Paul is the fallen soldier, the dead brother whose leaving is poignantly described in Merton's poem "For My Brother: Reported Missing in Action, 1943." John Paul's absence is reassumed into a new presence for Merton, a presence in memory and prayer and monastic life, a presence of a close one who has moved into the fullness of life which Merton experiences partially in his monastic existence.

The interweaving of the brothers moves in a gifted sphere not of their own making, from the earliest memory of fascination with the gift of new life, to the transformative inner spiritual presence of John Paul to his brother Thomas. In the power of change which grows and characterizes the relationship and their encounters, Merton exceeds his own framework of life and vision. He becomes aware in a personally transforming way of the good of creation, his sin, a free simplicity, and a depth of presence in absence. The

binding of the brothers, the drawing out of new creative possibilities in Merton's life because of the relationship, and the
movement of both binding and drawing into the future mark the
interaction as an experience of God which grows.

The initial question of this section—what are the significant
human relationships which both mirror and evoke the autobiographer's history of the experience of God?—presents an area for
attention, which can draw the reader of spiritual autobiography
more deeply into the life story of others.

9. *What is the deep desire for God which represents the moving force
propelling the life story forward?*
There is one God, but the autobiographies speak of many
experiences of God. The autobiographies describe those many experiences, as we have seen, from many different perspectives: in
"big words" which symbolically cluster personal experiences; in
experiences of personal change or conversion; in the correlation of
inner and outer experience; in relationship to a universal Chris-
tocentric referrant; in the immanence and transcendence of grace; in
a shifting image of God reflected in a shifting style of prayer; in
selecting out pivotal experiences; in human interpersonal relationships and encounters. The final question for a critical reading of
spiritual autobiography touches on the continuous moving force
which propels the life stories forward—the desire for God.

All people who tell their spiritual story, and certainly in a
particularly striking way the four people we have used as examples,
speak of their lives as a searching journey. The energy that keeps
them moving on their journeys is an intense desire for God. They
not only find the resource for continuing to search in their desire for
God, but in fact they find God in their longing. Psalm 42 is a
paradigm of this process. The Psalmist prays, "Athirst is my soul
for God, the living God. When shall I go and behold the face of
God?" (v. 3) Later the Psalmist says, "Why are you so downcast, O
my soul? Why do you sigh within me? Hope in God! For I shall
again be thanking him, in the presence of my savior and my God."
(v. 6) In prayer, the very longing of the Psalmist is transmuted into
the discovery of God as hope. So too, for the autobiographers, the
discovery of God takes place not simply in particular moments of
discovery, in certain instances, and in certain relationships not even
simply in developing lines of discovery, but in the very moving

force of their desire. The consequences for reading autobiography are clear.

The reader of autobiography who wants to appropriate the autobiographer's experience must come to share in that deeply rooted and dynamic force of desire to see God. Nothing less than sharing in the "thirst" expressed in the written record of life will afford the opportunity to enter the realm of another's experience. Practically, this means reflective meditation on the person's life story perhaps only at the end of the reading process. For the desire for God is the universally shared moving force for the unfolding of a life story, but the longing, in its shape and configuration, will emerge differently for different people. Furthermore, the particular pattern of desire for God may only be evident in light of the whole autobiography. Two examples of such reflective analysis are offered here. The first considers Augustine, the second Teresa of Avila. The analyses represent possible interpretations of the basic desire for God in the lives of these two people. Although other interpretations are possible, the underlying reality is sure. At the heart of the life movement of the spiritual autobiographies is an intense and personal longing for God.

The pattern of Augustine's desire for God becomes clear in appreciating the overall structure of the *Confessions*. Augustine molds his autobiography in a convergent structure of introspection and prayer. He looks within and describes his life as a series of events, relationships, and inner processes. He is not, however, merely reporting. He addresses his story to God in a prayer of many forms, sometimes as a narrative prayer, at other times as a paean of thanksgiving, and still at other times as a set of reflective musings and questions. The convergence of prayer and introspection signals Augustine's discovery of God within himself. The structure of prayer-introspection, and its significance as the discovery of God within provide a key for reflecting retrospectively on Augustine's journey.

The movement of his life has centered around himself. He is the young man searching for self-understanding, trying to piece together the puzzle of his own existence in a surrounding world. He is the young man seeking self-fulfillment which degenerates into petty and, at times, perverse forms of self-gratification. He is the young man who experiences self-alienation, an unrootedness of empty times and relationships with a measure of his own evil besides. Augustine's search is, in short, a search for himself. He moves from experience to experience by the sheer desire to find himself. A breakthrough occurs. In searching within himself, he continues to push within and, eventually, finds a reality deeper than himself beyond himself, yet within himself. He discovers a partner in his inner dialog, elusively present from the very beginning—God. Augustine's desire for God has moved his life forward. It has been, however, a longing in the shape of his desire to find himself. When his desire has led him to the double discovery of himself and his God, he could not more appropriately express his story than in a convergent form of introspection of himself and prayer to God.

Teresa of Avila also experiences a deep, moving desire for God. Her desire takes a different form than Augustine's. The key to her desire, which permeates her entire life story, becomes clear in the final phases of life described in the autobiography when she experiences ecstatic prayer. With rich imagery she describes her ecstatic prayer as the effortless pulling of her whole being body and soul out of herself into an utterly absorbing experience of God. After years of journeying, she experiences a prayer of closeness so encompassing and so deep that words can barely give indications of her experience. The desire for God that moves her searching into a time of discovery is a longing for intimacy, a desire to be totally absorbed into the totality of God. Retrospective reflection on her life story as the unfolding of the desire for intimate union with God pieces together some of the puzzling elements of her life. She is, for example, afflicted with many troubled somatic states, given to fainting, weakness, and a variety of pains. These states can be described as psychosomatic in origin. Perhaps psychological analysis could uncover the psychic mechanism which triggers her physical ailments. However, the reduction of the origin of her physical states to a cause-effect psychological explanation would fail to grasp the deeper dimension which triggers the psychic mechanism itself. For Teresa, as for all of us, the body in its physiology, and in the psychic mechanisms which govern physiology, functions as a symbolic vehicle of aspiration which transcends the limits of bodily space and bodily time. Teresa's troubled somatic states, then, represent her desire outpacing her body. When, in fact, her desire and her longing meet fulfillment in ecstatic prayer, her body and its states are changed as they are drawn into the ecstatic prayer experience. In describing the ecstasy of union with God, Teresa does not, as we might expect, abandon reference to her body and dwell on the joys of spirit. She presents what happens to her in terms of vivid physical imagery. The body which has been the symbolic vehicle of her aspiration is now the symbolic vehicle of her discovery. Similarly, her relentless search for spiritual directors and frequent talks with learned people is motivated by the powerful desire for intimate union with God. Her exchanges with these people often leave her mind confused. She is disturbed, and disturbingly presents herself to readers as disoriented. Still, she persists in pursuing consultations. Again, it is a matter of desire outpacing the capacity of her mind to absorb and sort out what she hears. Once, however, she experiences ecstatic prayer and makes the discovery of intimate union, her intellect, as she describes it, is quieted and drawn into the experience. By reflecting on the deep, dynamic, and particular desire for God, we can appropriate "from within" the unfolding of her story.

Conclusion

The nine questions to be brought to the reading of spiritual autobiography obviously do not represent the only questions that are possible. They are samples of questions that enable the reader to pause and take the story on its own terms. Taking the story on its own terms means that the reader has minimized reading personal experience into another's story, and may have, indeed, appropriated and shared the other's experience. The enrichment for the reader does not occur in filtering a story through the reader's experience. Such an approach leaves the reader unchanged, because there has been no movement into another experience. Entrance into a wider world of spiritual experience demands attentive hearing of the experience and stories of others.

At the beginning of this chapter, the stories of the forest spoke of many ways of describing the forest. If we allow one way, which ordinarily will be our current way, not only precedence but dominance, then we are the poorer for it.

CHAPTER THREE

FAITH AND STORY

Introduction

The previous chapter treated the particular stories and their particular experiences of different people who spoke from their unique perspectives and in specific forms of expression. All this totals to a large number of specific differences. Augustine, Teresa of Avila, Therese of Lisieux, and Thomas Merton, examples we have consistently employed, represent a wide diversity of experiences across historical, cultural, and sexual lines. The emphasis on differences and specific experiences has been deliberate. The last chapter aimed to indicate a way of truly hearing others' stories by bringing sample questions to the reading of autobiographical texts. The critical reading of texts with questions endeavors to perceive as clearly as possible another person's different and specific story. Such careful and attentive reading strives to minimize the introjection of our own experience in the stories of other people. To the extent that we allow our own experiences to filter the stories, we remain confined within the boundaries of our own experience. When, however, we enter another's experience and truly "hear out" the story, we come to share in a wider world. The net result of critically hearing particular and different stories is to hear the stories on their own terms, and so be able to appropriate them. A need, however, still remains.

Once we have heard and appropriated particular stories, we need to relate those stories to each other. Only when the stories are related to each other, can we begin to locate them in the wider flow of God's movement in history, and in that same movement today in our own personal stories and those of others. Relating the stories of spiritual autobiography means searching out the unity of the stories and seeking some common bonds of synthesis always, of course, with a respectful sense of their diversity. In other words, we need a generalized, systematic framework for reflecting on the stories.

The development of such a framework, as one might suspect, is a dangerous but necessary enterprise. It is dangerous, because it can lead to re-imposing categories of our own experience which fail to match, and therefore to reflect, the particular diversity of the stories. The danger lies in producing a clear, coherent, and comprehensive framework which tags and labels experiences with reckless disregard for the lived experience. This is, of course, the problem of manuals of spirituality which can provide deductive clarity for what may or may not exist in reality. At the same time, the task of developing a systematic framework is not only dangerous, it is also necessary. Left in their specificity and diversity and particularity, the spiritual stories of others offer little hope of a wider and more general understanding. If there is no understanding, there is no possibility of translating the insights of experience into the idiom of practical possibilities for the growth of oneself and others.

The need for systematically organizing spiritual stories outweighs the dangers. The dangers, however, alert us to the qualified way in which a systematic framework ought to be organized. A helpful and experientially adequate system emerges as closely as possible from experience itself. The systematizer checks the results of organizational reflection with concrete instances. Furthermore, when the limits of system applied to individual experience form part of the conscious awareness of the researcher, there is less likelihood that systematic categories will be stretched and pulled to do more than they can realistically do. Finally, a sense of direction is important. The purpose of organizing experience is not simply to reduce and tag experiences but rather to see lines of unity and connection for practice, in other words, a return to the lived experience.

This chapter will employ a general notion of faith which flows from the stories we have studied and the traditions of Catholic theology. That notion of faith will be related to spiritual stories found in autobiography. The style of presentation will be more assertive than probative. Verification of the framework's validity follows in making references to particular stories and in noting ways in which it can be of practical help. Finally, the last section will try to bridge the relationship between spirituality as study, and spirituality as formation by indicating the connections between the study of stories and the ministry to stories. That conclusion will lead us into the next chapter with its particular focus on the formational aspects of spirituality in spiritual direction.

A final word of introduction needs to be said about the use of theology and theological terms in chapter two and in the present chapter. Earlier, in analyzing particular stories, we used theology and theological terms, because to hear the stories on their own terms meant entering into the theological framework in which they were written. We spoke, for example, of the immanence and transcendence of the life of faith in the instance of Therese of Lisieux, not because she herself used the terms but because her experience and expression of transformation flowed from a reality of spiritual experience which also grounds the theological terms immanence and transcendence of grace. To hear the stories on their own terms means to hear them in the theology, implicit or explicit, which is at the heart of "their own terms." The present chapter also employs theology and theological terms but with a different purpose. The focus now is to unify, to synthesize, to connect. Some of the same theology and theological terms will re-emerge in this chapter but in a different context. Now, we can begin this second reflective task of studying spiritual stories by examining a most general reality which unites and relates them, a reality captured in the word "faith."

Faith

"Faith" is a code word used to describe many experiences. People say "faith" and mean some sort of general trust with more or less determined religious content. People belonging to churches with highly developed credal statements say "faith" and refer to a clearly articulated body of doctrine. The variations are numerous. For our reflections, I take faith to mean *our gifted relationship with God*. The remainder of this section treats the meaning of this definition, and, by developing its meaning, also provides some verification of the definition itself.

Who is the God with whom one is in relationship? This is a fundamental question which cannot be ignored nor, in fact, fully answered. Current theological studies warn us against a facile use of the word "god." Are we talking about a monarchical god of popular conceptions who sits aloof on high, managing the world like a masterful puppeteer? Are we talking of a god of our own construction, formed and projected out of our own psychic life? Are we talking of a god dynamically present to the world, enmeshed in its struggles, growing in its pains? The question of God cannot be ignored. At the same time, the question cannot be fully answered. It is impossible to do a fundamental theology, a study of what is foundational to theology, each time we use the word "god." Perhaps we can answer the question in a limited way on the basis of the spiritual stories with which we are familiar.

Augustine and Thomas Merton spin out the stories of their lives as searching for something that has elusively, but ineluctably, beckoned their discovery. Teresa of Avila and Therese of Lisieux are on a quest to uncover more completely something already given. Both the men and women find what they look for, each, of course, in a unique way. Their discovery, however, converges in a common pattern. They discover that "something" as deeply loving and personal, yet powerful enough to satiate beyond measure any hunger they may have had, as beyond themselves immeasurably, but inextricably wound into the very fiber of their being, as pulling them outside of themselves beyond their predictable confines, but doing so with a gentle freedom that lets them be who they are. In the tension between love and power, distance and intimacy, attraction and freedom, these self-transcending people meet transcendence itself, their God. This is the God of their story, who is in such close connection with them in their particular stories that this God appears to take on as many faces as the people who are met. This is the God with whom one is in the gifted relationship called faith.

To understand faith as our gifted relationship with God, we must probe the meaning of "giftedness." The relationship is gifted, because it is rooted in God's self-giving. God freely self-discloses, self-communicates—how, we shall see later. That self-disclosure and self-communication amounts to an invitation to share life, indeed, to share in the very source of life itself. Analogues to human relationships involving self-disclosure fail to capture the unique sense of the faith relationship. A couple getting to know each other, falling in love, committing themselves to the shared life of marriage mutually nudge each other to a self-disclosure which opens doors for sharing life. In God's self-disclosure, there is no mutual nudging. God initiates freely, and, effects completely His self-disclosure. The infinite mystery of love, power, distance, intimacy, attraction, and freedom must be the ground of all other possibilities. If, then, God's self-disclosure is to happen, it is God who graciously and freely self-reveals. So, the giftedness of the relationship, at least from this perspective, corresponds to the fact that we are given the basis upon which we can enter the relationship.

A further question arises. How do we come in contact with this self-revelation of God which is an invitation to share life? This is an immensely difficult question to answer in a universalist context. If we assume that God self-reveals completely in the sense of revealing a definitive word which discloses God and God's design for us, and also in the sense of revealing God to the entire human family, then it is difficult to pinpoint with exactitude the ways throughout history and in the various cultural and religious experiences of humankind that God has indeed made this self-disclosure. Our response to the question, "How do we come in contact with the self-revelation of God?" is much more restricted. The response is made in the context of the Christian tradition of historical revelation and faith. Within that tradition, one can say that the revelation of God as self-disclosure meets people in several principal ways: through the written word of Sacred Scripture, through preaching based on Scripture, and through the life of worship and mission in the church community. But to reduce the Christian contact with God's revelation to these three moments can be quite partial and misleading. Greater specification is needed.

Scanning through the Bible for information, listening to an abstract sermon, or owning perfunctory membership in a parish hardly represents moments of contact with God's revelation as an invitation to share life. The Bible, preaching, and church life bear God's revelation in the measure that they bear the message as response to deep human issues. For example, Augustine, along with all of us in some measure, faced the excruciating limits of the human condition. These limits come wrapped in the ambiguities we face when we face life seriously.

Consider for a moment some of these ambiguities on various levels of life. For example, the natural world is good. It is enjoyable and to be enjoyed. Yet, that same world at times presents itself as hostile and inhospitable to human life. Natural disasters happen.

Another example of ambiguity is contained in the reality of human community. Human community is good; indeed, it is necessary for survival and provides a source of some of our deepest satisfactions. Yet, human relationships which found community are fragile. They break. The human community can also unleash destructive forces which make natural disasters appear to be feeble tremors. Another example of ambiguity is on the personal level. I experience myself as good. I find various pursuits worthwhile. I am happy to be alive. Yet, I can also experience deep alienation within myself, evil and dark destructive forces. The sense of inevitable degeneration and extinction in death looms over me.

When an Augustine or a Merton or we ourselves face the hard questions of limits and ambiguity, then the word of the Bible or of preaching or of a communal experience can bear meaning because it bears a response. That response is an invitation rooted in the self-disclosure of God who, in the face of limits and ambiguities, says yes. The limits are not immediately overcome. The ambiguities are not automatically settled. There is a trusting acceptance of the basic response which holds a present invitation to share life, and a future promise to share life fully. Another entirely different set of circumstances also reveals the contact with revelation in the same interplay of channels of tradition and human questions. Therese of Lisieux, unlike Augustine, did not face limits and ambiguities with dramatic force, at least in the earlier part of her life. Her "question" arose differently. She tasted goodness and wanted more of it. In response to this longing, Scripture, preaching, and community life could be the bearers of God's self-disclosure as invitation to the fullness of life.

Simply within the Christian context, contact with God's revelation takes a number of shapes. In general, it is mediated through words which strike a questioning, searching chord. When the invitation is accepted (it can also be refused), then the person has entered the gifted relationship with God. Now it is the shape of the relationship which needs exploration.

Once revelation as invitation is accepted, then a person enters into the gifted relationship with God called faith. That relationship has been variously described, but the most consistently used imagery has been visual. The shared life relationship of faith allows us to see things as God sees them. We experience a new horizon or standpoint for our knowledge and love. In short, faith allows us to begin to see as God sees. In a way reminiscent of the prophetic experience, the person of faith possesses God's enabling spirit which instills a new visionary capacity. Furthermore, there are particular aspects of the new relational situation of faith which give sight.

The relationship of faith is one, yet the aspects of faith are multiple. There are intellectual, trusting, justifying, and ethical aspects of the single faith relationship. In noting these aspects even briefly, we can come to some better insight into the meaning of the relationship itself.

Faith leads to knowledge, specifically, of the Christian fact as the self-disclosure of God in Jesus Christ. There is, then, an intellectual side to faith's vision. Thomas Merton, for example, in the time around his conversion to Catholicism narrates his story of coming to grips with the notion of truth about a contingent world, the idea of God, and Catholicism as a coherent description of God and the world related in Jesus Christ. Faith's insight also shares in a design or plan of God for the world and the self. Sharing in the divine perspective generates a trust and hope in the future, while calling for a stance of reliance in the present. Therese of Lisieux, for example, in the last period of her life experiences difficulty concerning the truth or cognitive dimensions of faith but is drawn into an intense experience of trustful reliance on, and surrender to, God's promise. The "eyes of faith" can also see God's goodness, human sin, and the way of standing right before God by sharing in the life of Jesus Christ through his Spirit. So, Augustine, the sinner, experiences in faith a new graced righteousness or, in theological terms, his justification. Faith also illumines human life and behavior, thereby challenging us and drawing us into new modalities of existence. This may mean assuming ethical responsibility in a new way, as it did for Augustine, or taking on a new mission, as for Therese of Lisieux, or commitment to a life dedicated to worship and prayer, as for Merton.

We began to explore the giftedness of our relationship with God in faith. Our reflections lead us to perceive that giftedness in the way God self-discloses and self-communicates and so gives us the basis for entering the relationship. The giftedness continues once the invitation to share life in the relationship of faith is accepted. For faith opens up a possibility of vision which exceeds our native capacity. It discloses our world, our history, our very selves from "the eyes of the creator." In brief, we can only return to the initial description of faith as our gifted relationship with God. Still, we lack something. We have developed, even if in a very limited fashion, the notion of the God with whom we are in relationship, the giftedness of the relationship, and something of the multifaceeted character of the relationship itself. We have not, however, explored how the relationship is ours, how indeed it truly belongs to us. The understanding of faith as our faith, as a truly human reality, is crucial for organizing and understanding the stories of faith.

If we accept the description of faith as our gifted relationship with God, then, in order to be true to our perception of faith, we must acknowledge that it is truly of God as gift and truly of ourselves as a gift received by us. The offer of faith as God's self-disclosure is foundational to the relationship. At the same time, human acceptance of God's offer is integral to entering the relationship. The acceptance moreover does not result from any compulsion. It is a free acceptance unimpinged by constraints of evident facts or force or fear, or anything else. Because faith is partial vision, a reality of the "now" that relies on future fulfillment, it is necessarily a free acceptance of, and response to, God's self-revelation. A number of consequences flow from the nature of faith as God's gift and a free human response.

Faith as gift of God based on God's self-revelation is a unitary gift. It is as single and simple as the one who gives, because there is a singular and simple identity between the one who gives and what is given. In contrast to the unitary simplicity of the gift, the human acceptance is complex and multifaceted. A changing receptivity conditions our capacity to receive the gift. This means very simply that we are creatures who experience freedom in shifting degrees, who exist in an historical or serialized context, who move in steps of openness, actuation, and consolidation. To recognize ourselves as such creatures means acknowledging the fact of stories with their complex weave of human development as the way we are. If it were otherwise, there would be no stories but simply a single event representing a single life.

The two-fold character of faith as gift of God and human

response is a mystery in the technical theological sense of the word. A mystery in its technical sense means setting the parameters of reality in such a way that to exceed the boundaries in either direction means moving off of the reality. For example, the mystery of Christ expresses the Christological reality that he is both God and man. The formula may raise questions but it does provide lines for demarcating the reality. Reduction in either direction of divinity or humanity signals a movement off of the reality. Similarly, the two-fold character of faith as God's gift and human response, sets the parameters of the reality of faith. To reduce faith either to a divine business unconcerned with human response or to a human construction in the process of human development exceeds the boundaries marked by the word "faith." The reality contained within the line of demarcation remains radically inexplicable in its unexpectedness, be it the reality of Christ or the reality of our faith. The inexplicability of the mystery in its unexpectedness simply restates its quality as gift, as grace.

These highly abstract reflections on faith as God's gift and our free human response may leave the reader gasping for examples, something definite and concrete to which the theory may be pinned. The natural approach is to refer once again to the reading of spiritual autobiographies. The stories of individuals embody a complex experience. The people of the stories are intensely aware of a giftedness and a givenness which is well beyond their own construction, even beyond their aspirations. They experience a new vision flowing from their relationship with God, a vision which enables them to perceive truth, to hope in a future, to assume the complex ambiguities and limits of their lives and to walk in new paths. At the same time, the stories they unfold belong to them. Their struggles, their achievements, their setbacks—all these belong to them. Their stories do not betray an alien force taking over their lives. Indeed, the more intensely they find God, the more completely they talk of finding themselves. Their stories are, in short, stories of a gifted relationship with God. It is of God, it is of them.

The four spiritual autobiographies can provide many examples of how faith as our gifted relationship with God is both of God, and, of ourselves. Of the many possibilities, two examples, one from Merton and the other from Therese of Lisieux, speak concretely of what we have considered abstractly.

Merton writes just before his public commitment to becoming a Roman Catholic:

> All of a sudden, something began to stir within me, something began to push me, to prompt me. It was a movement that spoke like a voice.
>
> 'What are you waiting for?' it said. 'Why are you sitting here? Why do you still hesitate? You know what you ought to do? Why don't you do it?' (page 262)

Merton hears a voice which in the context of his autobiography is in one moment the ripening of his own questions and a singular time of graced impulse. He experiences himself, but, as touched in a gifted way.

Therese writes of the time of her profession:

> Just as all those that followed it, my Profession retreat was one of great aridity. God showed me clearly, however, without my perceiving it, the way to please Him and to practice the most sublime virtues. I have frequently noticed that Jesus doesn't want me to lay up *provisions*; He nourishes me at each moment with a totally new food; I find it within me without my knowing how it is there. (page 165)

Therese, like Merton, describes an experience of herself. The experience belongs to her, an experience of dryness. Within it, even permeating it, she perceives a sense of her gifted relationship with God. Both Therese and Merton find themselves in these particular moments and, in finding themselves, find God moving in their lives.

We can conclude this section by listing some general affirmations and noting the work still to be done. Faith in general represents a name given to multiple experiences. We have taken it as a relational term. It is our gifted relationship with God. The relationship of faith stands unique on two counts. First, faith is unique as a gifted relationship which comprehensively involves human persons and engages them in the deepest levels of their lives. Secondly, faith is a unique relationship, because it is susceptible to an infinite number of particular configurations which correspond to the particular stories of people. What remains for reflection is a study of the levels of faith and its dynamics. A pursuit of the levels and the dynamics of faith leads us inevitably to appreciate, organize, and understand the stories of faith, as stories of relationships with God.

Levels of Faith

The relationship of faith represents a comprehensive human reality. That rather general statement means something simple. Faith touches every dimension of being human. Still, perhaps a suspicion we mentioned earlier may linger. Does not a spirituality which grows from the stories and personal faith of individuals amount to a "personal" spirituality or, more bluntly, an individualistic spirituality? The question is a good one. History, especially recent history, alerts us to the dangers and limitations of an individualistic spirituality. The response to the question leads us to explore the levels of faith which set the wider context, the comprehensive framework for spirituality and the stories of spirituality.

Before we begin to develop a "geography" of faith, two qualifications are in order. The first qualification regards the use of language. In describing the levels of faith, we will employ metaphorical language. For example, to speak of "levels" of faith means borrowing spatial imagery. The image which breaks down aspects of faith (the task of analysis) does not adequately represent the faith experience which is lived in a single unity. Even in the realm of analysis, the spatial breakdown does not represent the fact that the levels are only inadequately distinguished from each other. The levels are not rigid compartments. In fact, they represent overlapping zones. The second qualification repeats an earlier declaration. The style of presentation will be more assertive than probative. Our reflections on the levels of faith will move in the general framework of Catholic theology and personal observation. Some verification follows when the reader matches personal experience with the assertions made here and when, at the end of this section, we relate the discussion of the levels of faith to the experiences contained in the autobiographies. The statements of purpose and qualification permit us to begin to examine the levels of faith.

God touches people on three levels and so offers the invitation to enter into relationship and share life on these same three levels. In other words, faith as our gifted relationship with God is realized in three zones or levels of life. In the Christian context, the Bible, preaching, and the church community thematize, present, and interpret the possibilities for realizing faith on the three levels. Furthermore, the three levels, as we shall see, correspond to basic human needs and aspirations.

The first level is *personal*, *mysterious*, and *hidden*. In the deep reaches of my life, I must confront myself, face up to the ambiguities as well as the aspirations that mark my existence. I grapple with the personal sense of my own destiny, and, even before that, what presently lies ahead of that destiny in the form of pain, joy, fear, and security. I come to terms with what David Tracy has called the basic trustworthiness of my life. No one can tell me, no one can supply answers. I alone bear the mystery of myself with a solitariness so deep that it remains hidden from the view of others and sometimes hidden even to myself. I can describe this personal mystery, but, only in halting and inadequate words. Sometimes I envy poets who through image and song make some headway in revealing what I find myself so mute about. Here, in silence, solitude, and closeness I experience a personal, mysterious, and hidden presence which invites me and affirms me. An external word, a crisis, or something else may trigger the experience. It comes in a flash or stretches over years. It enters with great feelings of warmth or with the cool penetrating refreshment of a breeze. However it comes, the experience leads me to say "yes." I believe in myself. The zone of faith is within me. The object of belief is also myself, not my naked self but myself present to infinite love. I know exactly what Paul means when he writes, "Your life is hidden now with Christ in God." (Col. 3:3)

The second level of faith is *cultural*, *local*, *communitarian*. Something within us draws us outside of ourselves to share ourselves and to belong to others. It is what leads to marriage and friendship, to establishing villages and organizing countries. Particular cultures arise to provide the tools anthropologists later examine, tools for communication, for collaboration, for binding together what we intuit as an already incipient communality. Language and customs are sometimes the matrix for, and sometimes the results of, the search to be together. We wed ourselves to a land. Even if we do not own it, it is our locality, our situation in space which provides a focal point for gathering as family, or tribe, or city, or any of the other numerous configurations of human beings together. As we strive to form community on any one of its levels, we may advance. Or, we may regress under the shadow of a mysterious and shattering social chaos that threatens dispersion and disorder. The need for community is so strong that human ingenuity builds intricate defenses of law, political order, myths, and customs to stave off whatever would harm or disrupt it. It is a story of pathos—of trying, striving, sometimes succeeding for a while, sometimes failing completely. In the midst of these efforts, an invitation arrives. In the Christian tradition, it is a convocation or a congregation, an act of gathering. The invitation offers a promise of relationship with the one in whom everything finds its unity. In and through that single relationship, the possibility of community finds a grounding power which enables human relationships and interactions to find their authentic level. At that point, we profess that we believe in each other. The object of faith coincides with the zone of faith. It is our community. We do not, however, simply believe in the product of our association. A deeper movement works among us. For, our community progressively grows into the very unity of the God of community, Father, Son, and Holy Spirit. Words of Paul come to mind, ". . . . we though many, are one body in Christ and individually members one of another." (Rom. 12:5)

The third level of faith is *global*, *cosmic*, *transhistorical*. The first two levels of faith respond to obvious human needs of self and of community. The third level also responds to a deep human need which is real but unnamed in a single word. Perhaps the lack of a single name indicates the incipient character of our consciousness of the need. It is a need which ordinarily does not stand in the forefront of our daily awareness. It is the yearning of individuals and communities to move toward global unity, eventually to be in communion with the entire cosmos beyond earth. It is the longing to cross lines of time and to be in relationship to the past and to the future. Only a few visionary people, such as Pierre Teilhard de Chardin, probe the meaning of this most expansive desire for relationship. When they do, they fire the imagination of people—a sign that a sensitive chord has been struck. Again, in this yearning an invitation arrives. The invitation presents the possibility of fulfilling global unity and cosmic communion, of being in contact with our historical rootedness and a future ahead of us. We believe in the world and its history. The accepted invitation of faith interpreted by the Christian tradition situates us in relationship to the Creator of the world and the cosmos, the Lord of history's past and future. Once again, Paul captures this movement when he writes: "In him everything in heaven and on earth was created, things visible and invisible." (Col. 1:16)

The three levels of faith, personal, communitarian, and global-cosmic, can be re-situated and synthesized in their Christocentrism. On the personal level, the believer recognizes the personal presence by a gift of the Spirit of the crucified and risen Jesus Christ, the personal savior who hands his life over for me and thereby meets and exceeds my desire to be loved. On the community level, believers gathered, again, by the power of the Spirit, experience themselves as individuals drawn together in a unity of life as "members" of the body of Christ. On the cosmic-global level, individuals and communities identify themselves with the full sweep of the world, the cosmos, and all history into a life of unity and fulfillment in the cosmic Christ, the glorified one drawing all creation into fullness.

Still another way of understanding these three levels of faith is to look at centering and focusing moments which we call prayer. Three major styles of prayer in the Christian tradition correspond to the three levels of faith. Global-cosmic-transhistorical faith finds its centering and focusing and expressive moment in the core liturgical-scriptural public worship of the Church. Although there are infinite varieties of liturgical forms, which we will consider shortly, there is a singular core of liturgical-scriptural worship which expresses a universal or global identity, a sense of worldwide communion in worship. The liturgy also connects itself to "heavenly worship" and a worship of cosmic proportions which relates believers to all creation. Finally, since the core of liturgical worship draws from the memory of God's actions and future promise, liturgy situates its participants in the full flow of history.

The prayer of the local and culturally-rooted community finds its expression in the particular determinations of public liturgical life, devotions, and religious customs which belong peculiarly to this community. The localization of prayer with its shared symbols expresses and facilitates the sense of belonging to a united community.

Finally, the prayer expression of personal faith is quite simply personal prayer, the inner dialog and reflection of the believer. The personal quality of this prayer with its searching and discovery matches the setting of the interiority of the personal faith experience.

The individual levels of faith and their corresponding prayer expressions leave us with three discrete and apparently unrelated levels. In fact, this is not so. The levels function well only when they are in a living relationship to each other. History tells us that when individuals or communities are fixed on or locked in one particular level, deformations take place. When, for example, a community fixes its identity in a one-sided universalist commitment corresponding to the global-cosmic-transhistorical level there follows a passion for standardization in faith life with exaggerated demands for adherence to doctrinal statements (not simply doctrines but their propositional formulation) and an institutionalism which rides roughshod over the community and personal levels. When a local community locks into its own local and cultural life without regard for the other two levels, the community can fall prey to sentimentality, particularism, or the kind of enthusiasm described by Ronald Knox. This approach isolates both the community and individuals within it from a wider horizon and from an intense and deep personal experience. When individuals isolate themselves in their own personal faith experience, deformations also occur. People walk endlessly with consuming self-consciousness down the corridors of their interiority. The classical syndrome of Quietism can occur; people situate themselves in an inward passivity which misses the wider ranges of the faith experience.

All these deformations point to a single need. Faith as our gifted relationship with God, a relationship which comprehends the totality of being human, must be lived on all levels. When individuals and communities experience the various levels of faith as flowing into each other, and so enriching each other, then they are living the faith relationship in its authentic potential as a comprehensive human reality.

The four autobiographies we have used as examples of spiritual stories illustrate how the levels of faith are integrated and develop in the lives of individuals. Obviously, the levels must be taken in an elastic sense when they are applied to individual instances. The levels signify some general categories which never match the lived experience exactly. Nonetheless, a reading of the autobiographies verifies the interplay of the levels of faith in the authors' spiritual stories.

Thomas Merton, for example, with his cosmopolitan background and travelling experience finds himself involved in a series of questions and searches in the world. He comes to reckon with these as he enters into a community of faith in the Roman Catholic Church in New York. Eventually, the community experience intensifies and develops into his entrance into monastic life. At the end of *The Seven Storey Mountain*, we find Merton in community and meeting the wider issues of world and cosmos, but now focusing on his personal discovery of God in contemplation. The order of emphasis and development differs for Therese of Lisieux. Her family and local community experience form her starting point. As she grows, she discovers the meaning of personal encounter with God. By the end of her life, she is deeply involved in community and her personal relationship with God but now with an emphasis on her mission, her outreach to a larger world. Again, the order differs for Teresa of Avila whose personal quest for God in prayer leads her to local community reform and involvement. Eventually, she works for reform with a wider set of Church concerns. Augustine, like Teresa of Avila, begins with a personal quest and discovery. This leads him to enter a community of faith. In the *Confessions* he then "cosmicizes" his experience by philosophical reflection on God, the self, and the world. At the end of the *Confessions*, he includes a commentary on the creation of the world.

From these indications, it is clear that the various levels of faith enter into the development of the spiritual stories. When all three levels enter a spiritual story, there is a certain wholeness or healthiness or authenticity about the specific life of faith. Furthermore, the interplay of various levels of faith indicates something very important about the nature of these stories. Their scope is wider than the personal history of the persons writing or telling the story. By drawing in community experience and universal concerns, the

stories represent a unique synthesis of individual persons who crys-
tallize the larger spiritual stories of their particular communities,
the world, and the very movement of history.

This section has presented a geography of faith—where the
faith response or faith relationship may be found. The various
levels, global-cosmic-transhistorical, local-cultural-communitarian,
and hidden-personal-mysterious, represent the zones in which faith
stories unfold. The next section on the dynamics of faith development will attempt to portray the way in which the stories unfold.

The Dynamics of Faith Stories

A full description of the dynamics of faith requires a massive
task of research and lengthy exposition. Some areas of research and
exposition might include historical studies especially of the Fathers
of the Church, theological studies on the role of the Holy Spirit,
and an interdisciplinary study of systematic theology and contemporary psychology. The scope of this section is much more modest.
The reflections on the dynamics of faith chart out pivotal moments
in the development of faith stories of people. Simply noting the
basic movements in the lives and stories of people without concen-
trated attention to causes enables us to see some fundamental patterns. The dynamics of faith, in this sense, arise from the stories
and provide a tool with which one can return to the stories for
synthesis and fuller understanding.

On the basis of spiritual stories and of a somewhat traditional
systematization of spirituality, a triad of sequential moments captures the movement of the faith relationship as a developing reality.
The triad is openness, actuation, and integration. A moment or
period of openness readies an individual by removing obstacles or
resistances and creating a climate of receptivity. The time of openness leads into a time of actuation, when something happens. The
something may be insight or decision or something else. Whatever
it represents, the moment of actuation infuses new life in one's
personal situation. Actuation needs integration. Whatever new life
or coming alive in a new way has been experienced must be drawn
into already existing structures and spheres of life. Then, what

openness has prepared for and what actuation has made happen becomes integral to the life of a person.

The triad as described here holds no charm and probably does not resonate with the reader's experience. The reason for this is that the triad as presented represents an abstract skeleton which in fact never appears except clothed in flesh and blood. There are three ways the skeletal structure takes flesh in spiritual stories: in a fundamental way, in an ongoing way, and in a vocational process.

The triad of openness-actuation-integration takes shape in a fundamental way in a basic searching-finding-consolidating process which centers on the act of faith or the moment of entry into our gifted relationship with God. Augustine's conversion provides a good example of the dynamics of faith in a fundamental way. For a period of his early years Augustine's life, with its restless flitting from movement to movement, presents a clearing or opening process. He experiments with philosophical ideas and religious movements finding one less soul-satisfying than the other. He confronts the limit situation of death which overtakes several of his friends. Again, there is a clearing, an openness. Then, in one moment, Augustine experiences the compelling call to believe. He says yes. An infusion of new life occurs as he accepts Christian baptism. It is a moment of actuation. The movement, however, does not stop here. It continues as Augustine draws into his already existing life and life style the newness of faith. He begins to integrate his act of faith into a coherent and persistent life style which reflects the new reality at work in him. In a fundamental way, Augustine's movement of conversion embodies the dynamic of openness-actuation-integration.

When the faith relationship already exists, when there is no question of coming to an act of faith as entrance to the relationship but rather of living in that gifted relationship, the triad of faith's dynamics takes shape in an ongoing way, that is, ongoing to the life of faith. Openness-actuation-integration again provide the skeletal movement but interpreted more precisely in the traditional ascetical-mystical theology as purification-illumination-union. Teresa of Avila's life follows the dynamics of an ongoing faith life development not exactly in a rigidly sequenced way but in a basic pattern of succession. She directs her efforts particularly in her earlier years toward a preparation for the intense union with God which she so desires. Her preparation in the form of ascetical practices of detachment from earthly things and consultations with many directors and books of prayer signifies her movement into an expanded freedom. When her life is cleared of certain resistances and obstacles, she experiences a process of purification for freedom which leads to her openness or readiness to receive the Lord in prayer more intensely. Eventually after many years, she experiences the actuation of new life within her as intense illuminations in ecstatic prayer. On a continuum with these experiences of actuation-illumination is the experience of union with God. The moments of actuation fund a wider experience of union which she begins to integrate into her life and into her communion with other people, particularly in her community. While the actuation-illumination experiences leave her at times dysfunctional, her progressive integration of union with God, by her own admission, allows her to pursue the routine tasks of life but now in a different key. In short, Teresa already finds herself in the gifted relationship of faith. The general dynamic of her life is not embodied in a conversion process. Rather, Teresa's movement follows openness-actuation-integration as purification-illumination-union.

A third way in which the dynamics of faith are enfleshed is in a vocational process. Although it is true that certain general patterns mark the life of faith, such as the call to believe and a general pattern of development, still there is a specificity, a "this-ness, " which is also integral to our gifted relationship with God. This specificity of the lived relationship translates the dynamics of faith development into a triad of availability-decision-appropriation. The history of Therese of Lisieux's vocation fills many pages of her autobiography. She provides an apt example of the dynamics of faith in a vocational process. Note, however, she also moves in the dynamics of purification-illumination-union, even though the shape of her ongoing development differs significantly from Teresa of Avila. In light of her vocational process, the time of openness for Therese unfolds in her family and early prayer experiences. She opens herself in a progressive generosity conditioned by early losses of her mother in death, of her sisters to the convent, of her girlhood in adolescence. Her progressive openness becomes a wider and wider availability to whatever her gifted relationship with God implies. She experiences a time of actuation when she receives a call to enter the Carmel of Lisieux and decides to accept the call. Then, in earnest, not simply in the playful aspiration of her early girlhood, she persistently pursues the decision. She clears obstacles to her entrance. Eventually, she begins and continues the religious life. Therese, then, integrates her moment of actuation-vocation by more and more appropriating the sense of her life as a Carmelite nun, until she reaches a unity of her life in love, and an overflow of that love directed to her community and a wider communion with a loveless world. The dynamics of faith are once more evidently operative in Therese's life but in a vocational process which marks the specificity, at least on one level, of her faith life.

To conclude this section, we ought to stop and resituate the line of our reflections. In the previous chapter, we pursued in some detail ways of truly hearing the specific spiritual stories of individuals. Deliberate efforts are required to follow a critical reading of autobiography without introjecting our experience on another person. The present chapter has a related but different purpose. Once the individual stories are heard, how can they be brought together? How can some synthetic understanding flow from individual stories, while the reader still respects their individual character? The search for unity led us to faith in its relational sense (our gifted relationship with God) as foundational to all the spiritual stories of autobiography. If spiritual autobiographies represent stories of faith, then an exploration of faith with the stories in hand provides a continuous unifying focus for understanding and, eventually, for practice. Our pursuit of faith led us to explore the various levels on which faith and faith stories unfold. The levels are global-cosmic-transhistorical, local-cultural-communitarian, and hidden mysterious-personal. A further question arose about the dynamics or the movement of the development of faith and faith stories. This led us to examine the general dynamism of faith as openness-actuation-integration as specified in ways which are foundational, ongoing, and involved in a vocational process.

The net result of the work thus far is a set of suggestions for the study of spiritual stories individually, and reflection on spiritual stories as demonstrating a certain unity in their relational character. All this represents tools for analysis and synthesis, for hearing and understanding—the task of spirituality as study. Now, we can begin to build a bridge to the next phase, spirituality as formation.

Ministry to Stories of Faith

This section and the subsequent chapter hinge on a basic conviction. Spiritual stories belong not only to the past but also to the present. There are as many stories of spirituality as there are people who try to walk by the Spirit. Only a very small fraction of the stories appear in print or even on a written page. A few more, but not many, are spoken aloud. The stories nonetheless live, each one particular and personal in its shape, all of them related to each other in their singular focus of the relationship of faith.

The spirituality of the autobiographies we have considered calls for analysis and understanding, a process of study. The spirituality of the stories being lived out now calls for a ministry, a task of formation. The ministerial function simply signifies a service to be rendered to people in assisting them to articulate and to understand their own stories of faith. Such service involves a formational task. Formation here does not mean imposition from without or shaping in a particular predetermined form. Rather, it means providing the helps of accompaniment, language, and other experiences, so that people may form or give shape to their stories and to their future direction. A question of value and purpose needs answering before we can pursue the sense of ministry to the stories of faith.

What is the value of articulating and trying to understand one's faith story? From another perspective, what is the purpose of a ministry to the faith stories of people? A response to these questions invites us to return to the reason for the writing of autobiographies. We noted a number of external reasons that are possible, but deep within each one of us there resides a need to gather together who we are, to affirm what our life means, and also to negate those elements which call for disassociation. The autobiographical act exercises our basic human freedom, not in determining conditions of life which are often simply given but in responding to ourselves. The articulation of one's faith story, then, means taking to oneself what is already given as life in its fullest sense. It is the fuller appropriation of who we are as loved creatures related to God and to one another. Similarly, the attempt to understand the faith story we have articulated draws us into a wider integration in the tradition of faith. We are enabled to move out of our own situation and discover lines of relationship with others who share the same faith in a different way. We further come to appreciate our own story not simply as a statistical instance but as a unique moment never duplicated in the movement of all creation into God. These brief reflections provide us with some sense of the value of articulating one's faith story and the purpose of ministry to these stories. Now what remains to be explored is the type of ministry to the articulation and understanding of faith stories.

In general, the ministry to stories amounts to a process of assistance or facilitation offered to individuals and, at times, to communities, so that they can speak their stories and understand them. Help is often needed because of the presumptions behind speaking and understanding. No one speaks a story unless the story's material has been sighted. In other words, help is needed to reflect and so to see what has happened. Indications, for example, of "big words," or conversions, or the correlation of inner and outer life, or a shifting image of God in prayer, or desires—all these can give a perspective for helping a person to see a faith story present in life. The process reverses the approach to the study of the autobiographies. The sample questions of chapter two are brought to stories already told. The same sample questions can be brought to stories yet untold to begin to gather material.

A further presumption lies behind the articulation of a personal faith story. A story must be told in appropriate language. Words themselves generate patterns of thought, and formal structure (see Augustine's introspective prayer) can convey not only the story but to some extent recreate the experience behind the story. Help in finding the tools of expression, or appropriate language, can be a valuable resource. Again, this pattern reverses the process of studying autobiographies. In the study of autobiography, a constant question concerns the sense of the language used. The language and expression are given. The student of autobiography endeavors to understand how it appropriately expresses the author's experience. In the current situation, a person trying to articulate a story may not have the language to do so. Help in that case consists in assisting in discovering the appropriate language for expression.

Concomitant to the telling, or articulation, of a story is the process of understanding it. Again, the presumption behind under-

standing is the existence of ways of understanding. Helpful resources can be offered to supply ways of understanding the faith
stories, for example, the relational nature of faith, its levels, and its
dynamics.

These considerations of the kind of assistance offered in a
ministry to stories of faith lead us to examine more precisely the
tasks of such a ministry. The tasks are given in some detail below.
They will find even greater specification in the following chapter.
For now, it is sufficient to note that the ministry to stories involves
a complex set of tasks based on the double dimension of spiritual
stories depicted in chapters two and three. In light of chapter two,
the tasks involve a focusing on the particular story at hand. From
chapter three, the tasks involve a movement into a wider field of
understanding and contextualization.

The basic set of tasks which lead to a personal telling of a story
are the tasks of memory, interpretation, and prediction. We are so
easily lost in a myriad of details, encounters, relationships, and
feelings. In some sense, we are swamped in our own lives. A ministry to our stories involves many questions and probings, as we have
already noted in the sample questions of chapter two, but in all
those questions the essential assistance rendered is a work of memory, interpretation, and prediction.

The task of memory does not seek simply to facilitate the recall
of earlier events. Rather than treating the recall of the factual, it
stirs the person to remember the funding moments and events, the
ones that give us life. I can recall, for example, that I went to the
drugstore yesterday. That is a simple fact which I remember but do
not live by. On the other hand, I can remember deeply if someone
said, "I love you." I remember and live from that memory. So, the
task of memory aims not simply to sharpen a person's recall ability
but to remember deeply through questions and shared exploration
the elements of life decisively memorable for its living.

The task of interpretation finds its purpose in the present. The
written autobiographies we have cited represent more than collec-
tions of the past lives of people. The autobiographies are told in a
present moment, a now. From the present standpoint, from the
present experience, the autobiographers draw on the elements of
their stories. So, the task of interpretation exercised in a focusing
way assists people in articulating their stories by helping them to be

grounded in their present situation. Readers of spiritual autobiographies have noted that the basic life development in them is unremittingly straightline. They give the impression of distortion precisely because the facts seem to line up so nicely, so coherently, so inevitably. In fact, the straightline development results from the unitary vision of people living now, but, looking retrospectively and seeing from their present standpoint a unified development, a story. Ministry to the articulation of faith stories must facilitate a living in the present, the now, so that the past can be drawn together and interpreted.

The task of prediction means ministering to the articulation of a story by contextualizing the past told from the present but geared toward the future. An autobiography or any personal life story does not represent an entire life. The dead do not write. The story is one in process. The articulation of a life story forms an interrupted moment in process. The ministry of facilitating the telling of a story must include some way of encouraging a gathering of the past from the present perspective but in light of a future openness and hope. The ministry is one of prediction not as divining the shape of the future, but as presenting the future outcome as open to further development and located in an essential horizon of hope.

The process of understanding accompanies the process of articulating the story. Nonetheless, there are two different sets of tasks involved in ministering to stories as people try to understand them. The first set of tasks of such ministry to understanding is providing a reflective resource to relate the various levels of faith to each other, cosmic-global-transhistorical, local-cultural-communitarian, and mysterious-hidden-personal. Obviously, the words themselves will be used rarely, if at all. The point of ministry in relating the various levels is to avoid the danger noted earlier of fixing on one or another level, particularly on the personal one. Our lives stand in a complex weave of relationships. Our faith develops according to all the strands of the weave. A ministry to the understanding of stories gently sets perspectives which enable an appreciation of the entire weave.

A second set of tasks define the ministry to understanding the stories. These tasks of ministry speak to the dynamics of the story, how it unfolds and develops as openness, actuation, and integration. The faith stories follow their own dynamics, as we have already noted. The task of ministering to understanding the stories, then, involves ways of indicating or highlighting the process.

Conclusion

The chapter has attempted to show that spiritual autobiographies are particular stories about a single story of faith, God's relationship with people. When individual stories are truly heard in their specificity through study, then one can begin to understand certain convergent lines which relate the stories to a single involvement of the authors and ourselves in a story of faith. To understand the story of faith requires another process of study which explores the nature of faith, its levels, and its dynamics. The last section of this chapter noted that the stories continue in lived experience. They often go untold. A ministry of formation to these untold stories, a ministry based on study, can facilitate their telling. Such a ministry involves a number of tasks which in various ways reverse the process of study. What remains for the final chapter is to specify in greater detail the ministry to the stories of faith.

CHAPTER FOUR

SPIRITUAL DIRECTION AS MINISTRY TO THE STORIES OF FAITH

Introduction

In contemporary Catholic thought, "spiritual direction" carries a number of meanings and associations. For some, spiritual direction means a highly stylized and formalized relationship between a spiritual director and a directee. It is a vestige of past programs in seminaries and novitiates. Spiritual direction offered a kind of private tutoring in spiritual life by providing an agent of accountability and an advice-giver. The program of spiritual direction checked the quality of one's pious exercises, dealt with individual problems, and met individual concerns which could not be brought into an external forum. The experience of spiritual direction by many priests, sisters, and brothers has led them to reject it or, at least, seriously question its value. Spiritual direction, in their minds, can only mean an elitist resource reserved for those who are truly serious about their spiritual development, that is, priests, sisters, and brothers. It promotes a privatization of one's spiritual life, when in fact the direction of renewal in the Church points to a wider and more fully developed community sharing. It makes good sense to reject spiritual direction as a retrogressive practice which has been surpassed by the employment of professional psychological counselling skills and a more community oriented spirituality.

Another contemporary trend which seems to be growing has moved beyond the traditional conception of spiritual direction and beyond the negative assessment of it to view the core of spiritual direction or, as it might be more appropriately called, spiritual dialog as a valuable resource for spiritual enrichment. Stripped of its elitism and rigidity, spiritual direction offers a resource for de-

71

velopment. It need not center its attention on individuals individually. New formats of group involvement can expand and develop in a healthy way the possibilities for exchanging spiritual experience. Spiritual direction taken in a wider sense of helping people to find the spiritual direction of their lives does not restrict itself to seminaries or novitiates. All those pastoral situations, such as pre-baptismal catechesis, ministry to the sick and dying, the sacramental celebration of reconciliation, marriage preparation, all contain a need for people to reckon with the basic spiritual dimension of their lives. So, spiritual direction or elements of it can profitably enter the wider tasks of pastoral ministry.

Our reflections on spiritual direction will lead us shortly to return to these images of spiritual direction both as a rejected element of the past and as a rediscovered resource for contemporary ministry. For the moment, it is sufficient to note these two general attitudes and also to describe a general picture of spiritual direction which represents a starting point for later developments.

The general picture, for now, centers on spiritual direction as a personal relationship. It involves two people, one of whom accompanies the other in a helping way. They dialog about issues of faith with attention to the personal history of the individual who seeks spiritual direction. The concern for the past, however, stems from a concern for future development. Both director and directee are committed to growth in faith life, a maturation into God's call to relationship. This general picture of spiritual direction enables us now to relate it to the ministry to stories of faith.

To situate spiritual direction taken in the sense just described next to the ministry to stories of faith as developed at the end of the last chapter shows a convergence of needs and a resource to meet the needs. The discussion of the ministry to faith stories outlined the scope of such a ministry as well as implicitly noting certain needs. Spiritual direction provides a basic need of ministry to stories, a forum for their telling. The unspoken but present question in describing a ministry to stories is: where can it happen? The process of spiritual direction offers itself as a place, a possible forum. The ministry to stories also implies rendering help, offering assistance. Spiritual direction concretizes that help in a director who functions as a reflective resource for persons who tell their story. The director can mirror or reflect experience, offer a wider horizon for experience and provide tools for understanding. The ministry to stories, then, benefits from spiritual direction which can provide a resource to meet the needs of a ministry to faith stories.

The benefit also runs in the other direction. Spiritual direction can benefit from a model of story telling. We noted above that some people today intuit a certain value in spiritual direction and pursue it as directors or directees. Still, many questions remain about spiritual direction. Greater determination of spiritual direction is needed. After citing some of the questions about spiritual direction, we can return to the story telling model and see how it responds to these questions.

A first question about spiritual direction touches a fundamental issue. Although some of spiritual direction's material has remained constant throughout history, such as prayer, problems, and decisions, there is difficulty in specifying its overall scope. People eagerly enter a spiritual direction relationship, but then often wonder, "What am I to say? to expect? to deal with?" Good-willed directors who no longer regard themselves as God's agents of accountability on earth wonder themselves, "What ought I to expect from the directee? from myself? what is the goal of the process?" A second question arises from our expanded knowledge of human behavior and personality. In the past, many issues which today are clearly of a psychological nature fell under the domain of spiritual direction. Then, the question emerges today, "If psychological counselling deals with the total person in relationship to self and to others (presumably including God in the case of a religiously oriented counsellor), how is spiritual direction distinguished or distinguishable from psychological counselling?" A third question about spiritual direction recognizes the existence of various schools of spirituality, each claiming a certain approach and recommending certain methods. "How," one asks, "do you reconcile these various approaches?" Finally, a more pragmatically based question asserts itself. People who struggle with the multiple demands of general pastoral ministry and the challenge of basic evangelization look on spiritual direction as a luxury for a few, ultimately detrimental to pastoral ministry because it fosters individualism and taxes ministerial resources which are already spread out thinly enough. They ask, "Why bother with something that is not only questionable in its scope but also negative in its effect? Besides, who but a few 'already saved' are asking for it or even know that it exists?" These questions deserve serious consideration.

A model of spiritual direction as ministry to stories of faith can respond at least partially to these questions. The first question concerns the content or material of spiritual direction. Although traditional responses to the question of content include, for example, "our spiritual life" or "our life of prayer," they are still vague. To center the material of spiritual direction on the telling of one's story as an unfolding relationship with God and others focuses the content yet, leaves ample room for many of the particular issues connected with the story and with spiritual direction as it has generally been conceived. People, both directors and directees, have a central focus to talk about and in light of that can profitably speak in a contextualized way of prayer, current problems, decisions, and vocational commitment.

The distinction between psychological counselling and spiritual direction raises a complicated question. A full resolution which honestly respects the complexity of the issues is hardly possible here. A line of solution, however, develops in viewing spiritual direction in the story model. The psychological counsellor looks to the immanent possibilities of the person in counselling, the possibilities rooted in personality structure, emotional and physical history, and the current socio-cultural setting for human interaction. Within those immanent possibilities counsellor and client confront problems of functioning and avenues of self-development. Spiritual direction as story telling must respect those immanent possibilities and, at times, focus attention on them, thereby offering a kind of paraprofessional help in the measure that the spiritual director is capable of giving it. Spiritual direction, however, as the unfolding story of a life of gifted relationship with God passes beyond the immanent possibilities of the directee. It touches on the transcendent and often unexpected presence of another who draws us beyond our possibilities in relationship. Counsellors have access to this religious relationship but as it affects the person in counselling, not as the primary or specific concern of the counselling. It belongs to spiritual direction to assume the task of centering and focusing not simply on individuals but, individuals as touched beyond themselves in a story of relationship with God.

Joy!

✝

*As the Father has loved Me, I also
have loved you. Abide in My love.*

John 15:9

Sister Helene of the Cross, O.C.D.
Maryann V. Williams
**Solemn Profession and Veiling
Carmel of Danvers
August 26, 1978**

O STRONG LOVE OF GOD! I REALLY THINK
NOTHING IS IMPOSSIBLE TO ONE WHO LOVES.

OUR HOLY MOTHER ST. TERESA

The third question also touched on a complex area. The tradition of spiritual direction contains a variety of schools with different emphases on spirituality. How does one manage to bring together Carmelite and Sulpician and Ignatian spirituality, even before attempting to synthesize these schools on the level of spiritual direction? The complexity of the question, again, only permits us to view a line, albeit an important line, of a solution. The story model of spiritual direction because of its generality and rootedness in a universal framework of the Christian experience offers a possibility for synthesis. That it is general needs no explanation. The notion of people caught up in a story of relationship with God can encompass all the descriptive lines of various schools of spirituality. That it is rooted in a universal framework of the Christian experience may be less clear. Because of our emphasis on using examples of spiritual autobiographies in Christian history, we may have obscured the biblical roots of the story approach to faith. One can see that the Bible is formed as an ongoing articulation of the story of God's relationship with God's people. The experience whether of exodus or exile, or of the Spirit of Jesus poured out on a community, inspires the telling of the story of God and God's people. Not only the events and revelation embodied in the Bible provide a normative experience, the very process of experience flowing into an articulated story regulates and models post-biblical history. In short, the various schools of spirituality find a universal reference in the word of God contained in a privileged way in the Bible as the unfolding story of God's relationship with God's people. A school which promotes the faith development of people no matter what its particular emphases may be can find in the story model of spiritual direction an appropriate description of its task.

Finally, the objection to spiritual direction raised in some pastoral quarters is met by reflecting on the essential scope of pastoral ministry and the scope of spiritual direction in the story model. A simple statement of purpose for pastoral ministry often fails. "To save souls," for example, obscures the issues in its generality as much as it illuminates them. The tasks of pastoral ministry are multifaceted. Perhaps the best way to understand pastoral ministry is simply to understand the adjective "pastoral." To do, or to give pastoral ministry means to provide the Lord's pastoral or shepherding care for people. That care shifts its direction according to the needs of the people cared for. At times it involves challenge, or support, or consolation, or question, or affirmation. It includes action for, presence with, intervention in. In all its forms, pastoral care renders the loving care of God in human form. Spiritual direction in the story model assumes that same basic stance of care and, in fact, crystallizes moments of its unfolding by remembering the past works of God, noting the present call, and tending toward the promised future.

The objections to spiritual direction as fostering individualism, taxing ministerial resources, and as peripheral to Christian aware-ness do not refer to spiritual direction as such but to a restricted notion of direction and a rigid framework for its implementation. As we have already noted, spiritual direction in a wider sense, especially as ministry to the stories of faith, can enter into a number of pastoral situations and not simply as one-on-one dialog. We will, in fact, recapitulate the communal possibilities of spiritual direction in the story model at the end of this chapter.

We have linked together spiritual direction and the ministry to stories of faith. Both benefit from the relationship. The ministry to stories of faith finds a forum and a concretization of means and relationship. Spiritual direction with its questions and flux in ac-ceptability discovers a model in stories of faith, a model which serves to answer questions from the tradition and issues recently raised. The following sections explore ways in which spiritual direction is a resource and a framework for ministry to the stories of faith. The emphasis here is on a relationship between two individu-als, designated here as director and directee. The implications ex-tend to a wider community application. One final qualification ought to be added. In describing the process of spiritual direction as a ministry to stories, there is little reference to technical aspects of the relationship, how to do it. The main point of concern, at this time, is rather what happens.

Needs of Story Telling Met in Spiritual Direction

The study of the autobiographies of Augustine, Teresa of Av-ila, Therese of Lisieux, and Thomas Merton generates insights into these people, and spirituality in general. It also provokes us to engage in the same sort of autobiographical activity, perhaps not in writing destined for publication but at least in the gathering and telling of our story. Spiritual direction, as we have noted, can take the story telling model and provide a helpful ministry to those who wish to pursue their stories. We have some sense of this process, but it needs more explanation.

This section takes seven elements which represent particular needs or requisites for people to be able to tell their spiritual stories. The first three are important fundamental stances needed to do the personal story telling. The last four are elements of the process itself. A brief presentation of each need is followed by a description of the way the need is met in spiritual direction.

At the conclusion of these reflections, we shall have moved from the analytic and synthetic study of other persons' autobiographies to indications of a process for constructing or telling our own and a specification of the ministry which facilitates the telling, spiritual direction.

1. *Uniqueness.* Before I even begin to recount who I am and where I come from and what has decisively shaped my life, I must have some sense of my uniqueness. It has never been easy to resist borrowing the images and understandings of other people to explain ourselves. Today, in a mass produced standardized society it is more difficult. Ironically, I may sense my problems and questions as unique to myself wondering if anyone has experienced my pain. At the same time, I may consider the overall positive direction of my life a rather trite and commonplace scenario played out in thousands of similar ways every day. There is drama in my pain but none at all in the overall movement of my life. I carry a "lumped in" feeling that I experience walking the crowded intersections of the city or driving its jammed expressways in the rush hour. A story of such boring dimensions is hardly worth the telling. Before I can begin to gather my life together, I must have some sense of my uniqueness, that I am indeed different.

The spiritual direction process as a free and interested discussion facilitates the achievement of the basic stance of uniqueness. In an atmosphere of freedom and attentiveness, what uniquely belongs to me can find room to emerge. The freedom of the process means an unwillingness on the part of the director or directee to short-circuit the discussion by prematurely pinning categories on experience. Categorizing, even and especially in lofty terms, kills an embryonic uniqueness by putting it in a narrow, airless, and standardized box. To tag this as redemptive, or that as the alienation of sin, only stamps out another spiritual figurine on the assembly line. Free, non-categorizing talk is essential for a sense of uniqueness to emerge. Directors are personalized symbols of such freedom. Their attentive interest coupled with evocative questions drawing on decisive memories avoids introjecting their experience on another person. Just as studying an autobiographical text critically demands patient non-introjective reading, so too, the hearing of another person. The interest level of directors in listening further promotes the directee's sense of uniqueness and allows a fuller exploration of life.

2. *Trust*. Lack of confidence automatically paralyzes me in the face of any task. Lack of trust in my own basic life direction and its outcome totally immobilizes me before I begin to tell my story. I must have a basic trust in myself and in the outcome of my life story before I can dare to gather together its elements and articulate it. Surely, this frame of mind reflects a healthy psychological development. It also reflects a fundamental spiritual stance of trust in the life relationship God offers me and where it eventually will lead me.

Trust in myself both in the psychological and spiritual sense cannot be given to me. I must take possession of trust myself. The spiritual direction relationship, however, in the measure that it is developed in a climate of trust can facilitate my taking possession of self-trust. Again, directors can be personalized symbols now, of sustained confidence in my story. Directors can further establish a climate of trust by exercising their predictive task, concretely by presenting the hope which grounds both director and directee in a future gifted by God. The autobiographers we have studied took up the writing of their lives in process precisely, as we have seen, because of a hope in the direction of their lives and relationship with God. Their hope generated a trustworthiness about themselves, enabling them to confront their story. The same stance must be present today.

3. *Focus on the present*. When one reads the autobiographies we have cited, it is presumed that the authors make no apologies for

inserting little asides which keep drawing us into the present, the time of writing. They live and write very much from a present focused moment. This is also a necessary stance today if I want to develop my spiritual story. If telling my spiritual story were simply an exercise of reminiscing about the past, no particular focus would be necessary. In fact, the telling of my story is a spiritual activity of the present. It gathers my life together now in light of further commitment, greater mission, or a more intense thanksgiving. Furthermore, the unity of the story does not emerge simply by a dispersive account of disparate events. The interpreted unity of my life comes clear only when I view it and tell it attentively from my present standpoint.

The spiritual direction process contributes to the fundamental stance of focused attention to the present. The process itself is a focused dialog. Its very format helps to situate the material in the "now." Directors also assist this focusing by exercising their interpretative task. They do not interpret by laying categories on experience but rather by reflecting to the directee the convergence of past life and future hopes in the present moment. In so fulfilling their interpretative tasks, directors serve as witnesses to the directee of the unified intelligibility of the story being told. It does make sense. The theological underpinning of focus on the present refers to a belief that God has acted in my life. That action continues in the present drawing me into a future. To believe in God's present involvement demands attention to my present position and reading my past and future from that position.

The fundamental stances of uniqueness, trust, and focus on the present form a prelude to telling one's faith story. The stances also accompany the telling and develop in the process, especially if the process involves spiritual direction. Beyond fundamental stances, there are certain specific needs associated with telling one's story, needs which can be appropriately and helpfully met in spiritual direction.

4. *Means of retrieval.* Where do I begin? The process cannot happen unless there is a starting point for gathering together the elements of my life. It cannot continue unless there is some way of retrieving information, memories, and events. The process of spiritual direction by its very format of dialog presses my efforts to

articulate and return to important sources in my life. The dialog allows and enables the emergence of life elements. Directors play a special role in the process of retrieval. Through questions, reflection, summation, and encouragement to continue, they offer directees an ongoing stimulus to draw from their lives. The study of autobiography has shown that a self-propelling dynamic of retrieval is present. Events are sketched, relationships are described, and feelings are depicted. Attentive reading begins to discern that the dynamics of retrieval and selection do not happen haphazardly. Once set in motion, the autobiographer begins to develop a life story in unified lines which correspond to a life unity which becomes more and more apparent. Similarly, when I begin to develop my story in a spiritual direction process with the assistance of a reflective resource, the return to sources will become simpler as the lines of unity become clearer.

5. *A language of experience.* How do I say it? I find myself painfully inadequate to the task of explaining myself. Anything deep which touches my entire being cannot simply be isolated, pulled out, and laid on the table. I will always have to reckon with experience outpacing my capacity to articulate it. But somehow I must find the language to express what I have found if I am not only to gather elements of my story but also to tell it. The spiritual direction process contributes to meeting the need for a language of experience. Spiritual direction does not offer a pre-set vocabulary. If it engages in a jargony exchange, little happens except a self-congratulatory attitude about spiritual achievements. The spiritual dialog furnishes a setting in which experience is presented and then, through the back and forth of dialog, re-presented, until the expression somehow matches the experience more adequately. Directors offer an additional resource for language. They can draw on the language of religious experience in the Bible and in the tradition of spiritual writers. They can do this not in an imposing way but rather in a way that presents samples of how analogous experience has been expressed. At this point, it is clear that in the role of and the process of being a spiritual director there is a convergence of the study of spirituality and spirituality as formation.

6. *Ways of understanding internally.* To tell my story and even to perceive some lines of unity leaves me still unenlightened about its

meaning. There is a need beyond gathering and telling. It is understanding. The first level of understanding is an internal one. How does my story hold together in itself? The process of spiritual direction meets this need for internal understanding through sequences of dialog which represent the internal patterns of my story. When I receive reflective feedback on those sequences, and if the feedback resonates with my perception, I can come to understand what has happened and what is happening. It may be that the dynamics of faith as openness-actuation-integration in my particular configuration become the key to synthesizing and piecing together in an understandable fashion what I have said.

Ways of understanding externally. My life is not lived in isolation. My story of life in faith can hardly be disassociated from areas of reality wider than myself. So, I have a need to understand my story on its various levels. The dialog of spiritual direction inevitably introduces perspectives of a wider than personal reality in discussing community, cultural setting, church, and world. The director's very presence embodies a wider range of life than my personal, hidden, and mysterious processes. The director further facilitates the wider understanding by indicating the several levels of faith and helping me to see their inter-relationships.

7. *A return to the lived experience.* Once I have told my faith story, I must face the fact that the story goes on. The process of telling and understanding does not form a purpose unto itself. The entire process is directed to a return to the lived experience with a depth that comes from understanding. I need to make the transit from the spoken story to the lived story. The dialog of spiritual direction, if it considers the future as an essential context for discussion, includes implications for living. It indicates paths for crystallizing and focusing moments of the faith relationship in prayer, ways of deeper commitment in the faith relationship, and the overflow of the faith relationship into other life relationships. Directors who function not as facile advice-givers but as reflective resources also provide a challenge to return in a renewed way to the lived experience. Their challenge ordinarily represents a mirroring of the directee's self-challenge to live by faith, the self-challenge which follows insight into the ways God has acted and I have responded.

The story model of spiritual direction offers an opportunity to discuss particular issues traditionally associated with spiritual direction but within a fuller context. The issues of improving the quality of prayer, making a vocational decision, integrating a new apostolate, discerning particular situations or relationships, all these are not merely treated as individual questions but are situated more realistically in an overall pattern of life. The response to particular issues of living Christian life inevitably find a more genuine resolution if they are not taken individually but in a wider context of life movement.

The seven needs of telling one story and how they are, or can be, met in a spiritual direction process specifies in greater detail the relationship between ministry to the stories of faith and spiritual direction. We can conclude this section by briefly noting the requisites for those who assume this ministry.

The first and obvious need for directors is their ability to create and sustain a climate in which uniqueness, trust, and focus on the present emerge. They must furthermore be in touch with their own story of faith and so be able to recognize the intrusion of their categories on the directee. From their study and experience of spirituality, they will find within themselves resources for asking questions, providing a language of experience, supplying ways of understanding the story, and challenging the directee to live out insights gained in spiritual direction. Presumed before all else for director and directee alike is the fundamental conviction that God has moved in the story of an individual's life. The movement is gentle, free, and unobtrusive at times to the point of obscurity. Its presence becomes clear in a reflective process of gathering, telling, and understanding.

A Wider Context for Ministry to the Stories of Faith

A strong objection to spiritual direction is that it caters to an individualistic spirituality. In fact, this has been the case at times. However, it need not be. The examples cited in the seven needs are deliberately kept to the personal level, and so they are able to illustrate in a specific way the interweaving of spiritual direction and ministry to the stories of faith. In the tradition of spiritual writing, personal autobiographies are the most accessible form of telling stories of faith. The examples and the history of spiritual writing ought not to limit our vision of spiritual direction and ministry to the stories of faith.

The wider range for stories of faith emerges in the lives of communities. Each community bears a story of faith that can be gathered, told, and understood. The biblical model, of course, in the history of Israel and the accounts of the early Christian community portray the community story telling. The writers and redactors of the text provide a ministry to the community stories of faith. Sometimes it is possible to capture a national experience or a community-wide experience on a scale commensurate with the participants in the story. At other times, in fact, frequently the story of a community becomes focused and crystallized in a significant individual, for example, Moses or David or Paul. The modalities of community stories vary, but the essential process remains.

The contemporary possibilities for gathering, telling, and understanding a community's story of faith seem limited or, at least, not realized. Coming to terms with a community story involves a complex task. More is demanded of the minister to the story who must tap into a wider flow of movements and people. Contact with individuals, work with groups, reflection on events, all contribute to the material of the story. The same principles of study as attentive listening to particulars and understanding in viewing the faith relationship, its levels, its dynamics as well as the principles of ministry to the stories of faith apply to both individuals and communities but in different ways. The structure of community life and worship provide avenues of access to hearing and speaking the community's story. A detailed exploration and specification of this task remains to be reviewed. It cannot be done in the scope of our reflections. Here, we can simply give an indication that there is a context for ministry to stories of faith wider than individual lives. In fact, the general sense of pastoral ministry, noted earlier, demands a ministry not only to particular needs as they arise but a comprehensive approach which reckons with the past, present, and future movement of the community into a life of gifted relationship with God and, so, among members of the community itself.

In a certain measure, the study of the four selected autobiographies and the discussion focused on the ministry to individual stories of faith both contribute to the formation of an ecclesial or community perspective. Because Augustine, Teresa of Avila,

Therese of Lisieux, and Thomas Merton belong to a community of faith and represent the movement of God's relationship in the community, we have been enabled to study and assimilate their stories and be challenged to bring a ministry to the stories of others. All this already speaks of ecclesial involvement

Conclusion

The renewal of spirituality today involves a renewal of study and formation. We only grow in the measure that we understand our gifted life in the Spirit and commit ourselves to formative ways of acting on our insight. The scope of such renewal can be expressed much more simply. It involves learning to listen, to speak, and to understand God's life intertwined in our own. It involves moving along together in this process of learning but also helping or ministering to one another.

To live life more intensely, more really at its true depth of relationship with God, that is the ultimate purpose of sorting out and implementing the stories of paradise.

READING REFERENCES

Chapter One

References to the theological importance of studying the experience of spiritual writers may be found in Louis Dupré, "Transcendence and Immanence as Theological Categories" and the two responses to Dupré by David Burrell and Anne Carr in: *The Catholic Theological Society of America: Proceedings of the Thirty-First Annual Convention*, ed. Luke Salm (Bronx, N.Y., 1976) pp. 1–19.

For an assessment of some contemporary questions concerning spirituality see Josef Sudbrack, "Von Geheimnis christlicher Spiritualität: Einheit und Vielfalt," *Geist und Leben* 39 (1966) pp. 24–44. Sudbrack elaborates his concerns in a later book: *Probleme-Prognosen einer kommenden Spiritualität* (Wurzburg: Echter-Verlag, 1969).

Chapter Two

The following editions represent the texts of the four autobiographies used as examples in this chapter and elsewhere. Page numbers in parenthesis in the chapter correspond to these editions.
The Confessions of St. Augustine. Trans. John K. Ryan. Garden City, N.Y.: Doubleday Image Books, 1960.
The Collected Works of St. Teresa of Avila. Vol. I: *The Book of Her Life; Spiritual Testimonies; Soliloquies*. Trans. Kiernan Kavanaugh and Otilio Rodriguez. Washington, D.C.: ICS Publications, 1976.
Story of a Soul: The Autobiography of St. Therese of Lisieux. Trans. John Clarke. Washington, D.C.: ICS Publications, 1975.
Merton, Thomas. *The Seven Storey Mountain*. Garden City, N.Y.: Doubleday Image Books, 1970.

For a helpful article on spiritual autobiography especially from the historical point of view see: F. Vernet, "Autobiographies spirituelles" in *Dictionnaire de spiritualité ascetique et mystique*, Vol. 1, ed. Marcel Viller (Paris: Beauchesne, 1937) cols. 1141–1159.

Chapter Three

For the general notion of faith I am indebted to the masterful work of my teacher Juan Alfaro, *Fides, spes, caritas: Adnotationes in tractatum de virtutibus theologicis* (Rome: Pontifical Gregorian University Press, 1964). See also Alfaro's *Cristología y antropoligía: Temas teologicos actuales* (Madrid: Ediciones Cristiandad, 1973) especially the influential article "Persona y gracia," pp. 345–366.

On the levels of faith, Pierre Teilhard de Chardin's essay "How I Believe" is very illuminating. It is found in *Christianity and Evolution*, trans. René Hague (New York: Harcourt, Brace Jovanovich, Inc., 1971) pp. 96–132.

Some general and helpful material on the dynamics of spiritual development may be found in Louis Cognet, *Introduction à la vie chrétienne. I: Les problèmes de la spiritualité. II: L'ascese chrétienne. III: La prière du chretien.* 3 vols. (Paris: Editions du Cerf, 1967).

Chapter Four

There are many fine books and articles on spiritual direction. Here, I note two studies which I have found extremely helpful. The third study is a pamphlet I prepared for the Bishops' Committee on Priestly Life and Ministry; it touches on spiritual direction in a specific area.

Isabell, Damien. *The Spiritual Director: A Practical Guide.* Chicago, Franciscan Herald Press, 1976.

Laplace, Jean. *Preparing for Spiritual Direction.* Trans. John C. Guinness. Chicago: Franciscan Herald Press, 1975.

Cameli, Louis John. *Spiritual Direction for Priests: The Rediscovery of a Resource.* Washington, D.C.: USCC Publications, 1976.

A book which locates and exlores the wider community context of stories of faith is John Shea's recent and extraordinary helpful book *Stories of God: An Unauthorized Biography* (Chicago: The Thomas More Press, 1978). Shea develops at length what we have touched on in a cursory way.